PSALMS, HYMNS AND
SPIRITUAL SONGS

PSALMS, HYMNS AND SPIRITUAL SONGS

WHAT THE BIBLE SAYS ABOUT MUSIC

Second Edition

—⬥—

Donald Thiessen

CORNERSTONE PRESS CHICAGO
CHICAGO, ILLINOIS

Scripture taken from the New American Standard Bible, © 1960, 1962 1963, 1968, 1971, 1972, 1973, 1975, 1977 by The Lockman Foundation. Used by permission.

ISBN 0-940895-06-4
Printed in the United States of America.
97 96 95 94 5 4 3 2 1

Library of Congress Cataloging-in-Publication Data

Thiessen, Don.
    Psalms, hymns and spiritual songs: what the bible says about music / by Don Thiessen.
        p.   cm.
    "Scripture quotations taken from the New American Standard Bible."
    -T.p. verso
    Includes index.
    1. Music in the Bible. I. Bible   English.   New American
Standard. II. Title.
ML166.T45   1993
    220.8' 78—dc20   93-16044
                                                                      CIP
                                                                      MN

CONTENTS

FOREWORD

I have long been a fan of anyone who truly loves the Christian musician. Having chatted with the author/compiler of this book on several occasions, I am assured of his honest concern for those embarking on the musician's journey. Too few understand or take the time to work through the questions that a serious Christian musician must find solutions to if they want to serve God with their skill.

In this book Dr. Don Thiessen has provided the foundation for what we must do. God's Word is the essential source for our faith and practice. It is therefore with thanks to the Lord and to Dr. Thiessen that we gladly offer this help to all who are concerned about pleasing the Lord with their musical efforts.

In the words of A. W. Tozer, "Nothing less than a whole Bible will make a whole Christian." If that be true, it is no less true with regard to those verses that clearly, contextually speak to this issue in the Scriptures. Studying the Bible's own words about music is central to developing a mature theology of music. Alas, after nearly two thousand years the Church still is in want of one!

May this book bring the truth of God's commentary about music and it's use ever more into the hearts, minds, and lives of His servants.

GLENN KAISER

PREFACE

When as a teenager I became involved in the music of the church, any question I might have had seemed to have fairly simple, uncomplicated answers. I sang in quartets and choirs and led some groups with much joy and enthusiasm.

All this changed because of two things. One was the dramatic change in popular music and the subsequent developments in Christian music. To many these changes were not just bewildering but agonizing as traditional views of music were reexamined and challenged. Few Christians have been able to side-step these issues over the past three decades.

The second event was of my own doing. I decided to enter formal music studies at a secular university in preparation for a music teaching career. I saw not only unbelievers, but also believers who seemed to set aside the pursuit of holiness to pursuits in music. I was not willing to do this. Music and Christianity had to be compatible.

My approach to these conflicting ideas was to read the Bible to determine what music was for the people of God. I found it was to a large extent a joyful expression of praise to God. The Bible presented music as a positive activity, pleasing to God in almost every way. My continued study finally led to this compilation, which I used in my college teaching to encourage students to develop a philosophy of music ministry based on the Scriptures.

Those who are familiar with the first edition, *A Compilation of Scripture Passages on Music*, will notice some new features. The passages have been given headings, musical terms and musicians are highlighted, and the concordance is expanded.

My hope is that this volume will be helpful to those who need to refocus their concepts of music according to biblical principles. Also, I trust this will prove useful for those who wish to research specific aspects of music in the Bible.

DONALD THIESSEN

INTRODUCTION

This resource has been in preparation over a period of several years as I have personally sought to develop a philosophy of music that is biblical and realistic in the ministry today. The Bible gives some pointed directions on what music is to be for the people of God, but it still leaves many of the specifics to our discretion and judgment. As the text was important in the music of the Bible, so the text must be important to us. It is as we study the Christian's primary resource material, the Bible, that we can develop a theology or philosophy of church music that will be pleasing to God.

In my assignments to students over the years I have asked them to write papers on topics such as the following, using only the Bible as their authority and resource:

1. God's Response to Music
2. Man's Response to Music
3. Descriptive versus Prescriptive Statements on Music
4. Music and Worship
5. Solo versus Group Singing
6. The Paid Music Ministry
7. The Subject Matter of Bible Hymnody
8. Professional Performance versus Layman Participation
9. The Christian and Music as Entertainment
10. Instrumental Music in the Church
11. Interpretive Movement and Christian Music
12. The Role of Church Leadership in Music
13. Music as an Act of Witness
14. The Musician as a Minister

In using this material it is important that the student study the contexts of the passages to arrive at conclusions. Often there are broader implications than what is actually contained in specific verses.

I trust that as you use this reference material you will come to a biblically based philosophy that will make your ministry effective whether it is in music or another area.

EXPLANATION OF GENERAL FORMAT

MUSICAL TERMS AND MUSICIANS are highlighted in bold text.

PARAGRAPHS are designated by bold face number.

QUOTATION MARKS are used in the text in accordance with modern English usage.

PUNCTUATION CHANGES have been made to conform with modern practice.

"THOU", "THY", AND THEE" are changed to "you" except in the language of prayer when addressing deity.

PERSONAL PRONOUNS are capitalized when pertaining to deity.

ITALICS are used in the text to indicate words which are not found in the original Hebrew or Greek but implied by it.

SMALL CAPS in the New Testament are used in the text to indicate Old Testament quotes.

ASTERISK—Verbs marked with an asterisk (*) represent historical presents in the Greek which have been translated with an English past tense in order to conform to modern usage.

Part One:
Bible Passages

OLD TESTAMENT

GENESIS

LAMECH'S OFFSPRING

4:19–24   21 And his brother's name was **Jubal**; he was the father of all those who **play** the **lyre** and **pipe**.

JACOB FLEEING FROM LABAN

31:22–32   27 "Why did you flee secretly and deceive me, and did not tell me, so that I might have sent you away with joy and with **songs**, with **timbrel** and with **lyre**;

EXODUS

RED SEA CELEBRATION

15:1–21   1 Then **Moses** and the sons of Israel **sang** this **song** to the LORD, and said,

> "I will **sing** to the LORD, for He is highly exalted;
> The horse and its rider He has hurled into the sea.

2   "The LORD is my strength and **song**,
> And He has become my salvation;
> This is my God, and I will praise Him;
> My father's God, and I will extol Him.

20 And **Miriam** the prophetess, Aaron's sister, took the **timbrel** in her hand, and all the women went out after her with **timbrels** and with **dancing**.

21 And **Miriam** answered them,

> "**Sing** to the LORD, for He is highly exalted;
> The horse and his rider He has hurled into
> the sea."

GIVING OF THE COMMANDMENTS

19:10–20

13 'No hand shall touch him, but he shall surely be stoned or shot through; whether beast or man, he shall not live.' When the **ram's horn sounds** a long **blast**, they shall come up to the mountain.

16 So it came about on the third day, when it was morning, that there were thunder and lightning flashes and a thick cloud upon the mountain and a very loud **trumpet sound,** so that all the people who *were* in the camp trembled.

19 When the **sound** of the **trumpet** grew louder and louder, **Moses** spoke and God answered him with thunder.

20:1–26

18 And all the people perceived the thunder and the lightning flashes and the **sound** of the **trumpet** and the mountain smoking; and when the people saw *it,* they trembled and stood at a distance.

THE GOLDEN CALF

32:15–20

18 But he said,
> "It is not the **sound** of the cry of triumph,
> Nor is it the **sound** of the cry of defeat;
> But the **sound** of *singing* I hear."

19 And it came about, as soon as **Moses** came near the camp, that he saw the calf and *the* **dancing**; and Moses' anger burned, and he threw the tablets from his hands and shattered them at the foot of the mountain.

LEVITICUS

A CALL TO REMEMBER

23:24–25

24 "Speak to the sons of Israel, saying, 'In the seventh month on the first of the month, you shall have a rest, a

reminder by **blowing** *of trumpets*, a holy convocation.

ANNOUNCEMENT OF THE JUBILEE

25:8–12   9 'You shall then **sound** a **ram's horn** abroad on the tenth day of the seventh month; on the day of atonement you shall **sound** a **horn** all through your land.

NUMBERS

INSTRUCTIONS FOR SUMMONING PEOPLE

10:1–10   2 "Make yourself two **trumpets** of silver, of hammered work you shall make them; and you shall use them for summoning the congregation and for having the camps set out.

3 "And when both are **blown**, all the congregation shall gather themselves to you at the doorway of the tent of meeting.

4 "Yet if *only* one is **blown**, then the leaders, the heads of the divisions of Israel, shall assemble before you.

5 "But when you **blow** an alarm, the camps that are pitched on the east side shall set out.

6 "And when you **blow** an alarm the second time, the camps that are pitched on the south side shall set out; an alarm is to be **blown** for them to set out.

7 "When convening the assembly, however, you shall **blow** without **sounding** an alarm.

8 "The priestly sons of Aaron, moreover, shall **blow** the **trumpets**; and this shall be for you a perpetual statute throughout your generations.

9 "And when you go to war in your land against the adversary who attacks you, then you shall **sound** an alarm with the **trumpets**, that you may be remembered before the LORD your God, and be saved from your enemies.

10 "Also in the day of your gladness and in your appointed feasts, and on the first *days* of your months, you shall **blow** the **trumpets** over your burnt offerings, and over the sacrifices of your peace offerings; and they shall be as a reminder of you before your God. I am the LORD your God."

THANKSGIVING FOR WATER

21:16–18

17 Then Israel **sang** this **song**:
"**Spring up**, O well! **Sing** to it!

INSTRUCTION FOR ASSEMBLIES

29:1–6

1 'Now in the seventh month, on the first day of the month, you shall also have a holy convocation; you shall do no laborious work. It will be to you a day for **blowing trumpets**.

MUSIC IN WAR

31:1–12

6 And **Moses** sent them, a thousand from each tribe, to the war, and Phinehas the son of Eleazar the priest, to the war with them, and the holy vessels and the **trumpets** for the alarm in his hand.

DEUTERONOMY

THE LORD COMMANDS MOSES TO COMPOSE

31:19–22, 30

19 "Now therefore, write this **song** for yourselves, and teach it to the sons of Israel; put it on their lips, in order that this **song** may be a witness for Me against the sons of Israel.

21 "Then it shall come about, when many evils and troubles have come upon them, that this **song** will testify before them as a witness (for it shall not be forgotten from the lips of their descendants); for I know their intent which they are developing today, before I have brought them into the land which I swore."

22 So **Moses** wrote this **song** the same day, and taught it to the sons of Israel.

30 Then **Moses** spoke in the hearing of all the assembly of Israel the words of this **song**, until they were complete:

MOSES' LAST COMPOSITION

32:1–47

44 Then **Moses** came and spoke all the words of this **song** in the hearing of the people, he, with Joshua the son of Nun.

JOSHUA

THE FALL OF JERICHO

6:1–21

4 "Also seven priests shall carry seven **trumpets** of **rams' horns** before the ark; then on the seventh day you shall march around the city seven times, and the priests shall **blow** the **trumpets**.

5 "And it shall be that when they make a long **blast** with the **ram's horn**, and when you hear the **sound** of the **trumpet**, all the people shall shout with a great shout; and the wall of the city will fall down flat, and the people will go up every man straight ahead."

6 So Joshua the son of Nun called the priests and said to them, "Take up the ark of the covenant, and let seven priests carry seven **trumpets** of **rams' horns** before the ark of the LORD."

8 And it was *so,* that when Joshua had spoken to the people, the seven priests carrying the seven **trumpets** of **rams' horns** before the LORD went forward and blew the **trumpets**; and the ark of the covenant of the LORD followed them.

9 And the armed men went before the priests who **blew** the **trumpets**, and the rear guard came after the ark, while they continued to **blow** the **trumpets**.

13 And the seven priests carrying the seven **trumpets** of **rams' horns** before the ark of the LORD went on continually, and **blew** the **trumpets**; and the armed men went before them, and the rear guard came after the ark of the LORD, while they continued to **blow** the **trumpets**.

16 And it came about at the seventh time, when the priests **blew** the **trumpets**, Joshua said to the people, "Shout! For the LORD has given you the city.

20 So the people shouted, and *priests* **blew** the **trumpets**; and it came about, when the people heard the **sound** of the **trumpet**, that the people shouted with a great shout and the wall fell down flat, so that the people went up into the city, every man straight ahead, and they took the city.

JUDGES

EHUD SUMMONING WARRIORS

3:26–30   27 And it came about when he had arrived, that he **blew**
the **horn** in the hill country of Ephraim; and the sons of
Israel went down with him from the hill country, and he
was in front of them.

DEBORAH AND BARAK'S SONG

5:1–31   **1** Then **Deborah** and **Barak** the son of Abinoam **sang**
on that day, saying,

2   "That the leaders led in Israel,
That the people volunteered,
Bless the LORD!

3   "Hear, O kings; give ear, O rulers!
I—to the LORD, I will **sing**,
I will sing praise to the LORD, the God of
Israel.

10   "You who ride on white donkeys,
You who sit on *rich* carpets,
And you who travel on the road—**sing**!

12   "Awake, awake, Deborah;
Awake, awake, **sing a song**!
Arise, Barak, and take away your captives, O
son of Abinoam.

16   "Why did you sit among the sheepfolds,
To hear the **piping** for the flocks?
Among the divisions of Reuben
There were great searchings of heart.

GIDEON SUMMONING WARRIORS

6:33–35   34 So the Spirit of the LORD came upon Gideon; and he
blew a **trumpet**, and the Abiezrites were called together to
follow him.

GIDEON DEFEATS THE MIDIANITES

7:1–25   8 So the 300 men took the people's provisions and their
trumpets into their hands. And Gideon sent all the *other*

men of Israel, each to his tent, but retained the 300 men; and the camp of Midian was below him in the valley.

16 And he divided the 300 men into three companies, and he put **trumpets** and empty pitchers into the hands of all of them, with torches inside the pitchers.

18 "When I and all who are with me **blow** the **trumpet**, then you also **blow** the **trumpets** all around the camp, and say, 'For the LORD and for Gideon.'"

19 So Gideon and the hundred men who were with him came to the outskirts of the camp at the beginning of the middle watch, when they had just posted the watch; and they **blew** the **trumpets** and smashed the pitchers that were in their hands.

20 When the three companies **blew** the **trumpets** and broke the pitchers, they held the torches in their left hands and the **trumpets** in their right hands for blowing, and cried, "A sword for the LORD and for Gideon!"

22 And when they blew 300 **trumpets**, the LORD set the sword of one against another even throughout the whole army; and the army fled as far as Beth-shittah toward Zererah, as far as the edge of Abel-meholah, by Tabbath.

JEPHTHAH'S DAUGHTER

11:34–40

34 When Jephthah came to his house at Mizpah, behold, his daughter was coming out to meet him with **tambourines** and with **dancing**. Now she was his one *and* only child; besides her he had neither son nor daughter.

WIVES FOR THE BENJAMITES

21:19–24

21 and watch; and behold, if the daughters of Shiloh come out to take part in the **dances**, then you shall come out of the vineyards and each of you shall catch his wife from the daughters of Shiloh, and go to the land of Benjamin.

23 And the sons of Benjamin did so, and took wives according to their number from those who **danced**, whom they carried away. And they went and returned to their inheritance, and rebuilt the cities and lived in them.

RUTH

FIRST SAMUEL

SAUL PROPHESYING

10:1–13   5 "Afterward you will come to the hill of God where the Philistine garrison is; and it shall be as soon as you have come there to the city, that you will meet a group of prophets coming down from the high place with **harp**, **tambourine**, **flute**, and a **lyre** before them, and they will be prophesying.

JONATHAN SMITES THE PHILISTINES

13:1–4   3 And Jonathan smote the garrison of the Philistines that was in Geba, and the Philistines heard of *it*. Then **Saul blew** the **trumpet** throughout the land, saying, "Let the Hebrews hear."

SAUL ENGAGES DAVID AS COURT MUSICIAN

16:14–23   16 "Let our lord now command your servants who are before you. Let them seek a man who is a **skillful player** on the **harp**; and it shall come about when the evil spirit from God is on you, that he shall **play** *the harp* with his hand, and you will be well."

17 So Saul said to his servants, "Provide for me now a man who can **play** well, and bring *him* to me."

18 Then one of the young men answered and said, "Behold, I have seen a son of Jesse the Bethlehemite who is a **skillful musician**, a mighty man of valor, a warrior, one prudent in speech, and a handsome man; and the LORD is with him."

23 So it came about whenever the *evil* spirit from God came to Saul, **David** would take the **harp** and **play** *it* with his hand; and **Saul** would be refreshed and be well, and the evil spirit would depart from him.

WOMEN PRAISE DAVID

18:6–9   **6** And it happened as they were coming, when David returned from killing the Philistine, that the women came out of all the cities of Israel, **singing** and **dancing**, to meet King Saul, with **tambourines**, with joy and with **musical instrument**s.

7 And the women **sang** as they **played**, and said,
>"Saul has slain his thousands,
>And David his ten thousands."

SAUL TRIES TO KILL DAVID

18:10–11   **10** Now it came about on the next day that an evil spirit from God came mightily upon Saul, and he raved in the midst of the house, while David was **playing** *the **harp*** with his hand, as usual; and a spear *was* in Saul's hand.

SAUL TRIES TO KILL DAVID AGAIN

19:9–10   9 Now there was an evil spirit from the LORD on Saul as he was sitting in his house with his spear in his hand, and David was playing *the **harp*** with *his* hand.

DAVID FEIGNS MADNESS

21:10–15   11 But the servants of Achish said to him, "Is this not David the king of the land? Did they not **sing** of this one as they **danced**, saying,
>'Saul has slain his thousands,
>And David his ten thousands'?"

DAVID, ACHISH, AND THE PHILISTINES

29:1–5   5 "Is this not David, of whom they **sing** in the **dances**, saying,
>'Saul has slain his thousands,
>And David his ten thousands'?"

DAVID RESCUES HIS WIVES AND GOODS

30:16–20   **16** And when he had brought him down, behold, they were spread over all the land, eating and drinking and **dancing** because of all the great spoil that they had taken from the land of the Philistines and from the land of Judah.

SECOND SAMUEL

DAVID SORROWS FOR JONATHAN

1:17–27

17 Then David **chanted** with this **lament** over Saul and Jonathan his son,

18 and he told *them* to teach the sons of Judah *the* **song** *of* the bow; behold, it is written in the book of Jashar.

JOAB PURSUES ABNER

2:24–29

28 So Joab **blew** the **trumpet**; and all the people halted and pursued Israel no longer, nor did they continue to fight anymore.

DAVID SORROWS FOR ABNER

3:31–39

31 Then David said to Joab and to all the people who were with him, "Tear your clothes and gird on sackcloth and **lament** before Abner." And King David walked behind the bier.

33 And the king **chanted** a *lament* for Abner and said,
"Should Abner die as a fool dies?

VICTORY CELEBRATION BY DAVID

6:1–23

5 Meanwhile, David and all the house of Israel were celebrating before the LORD with all kinds of *instruments made* of fir wood, and with **lyres**, **harps**, **tambourines**, **castanets** and **cymbals**.

14 And David was **dancing** before the LORD with all *his* might, and David was wearing a linen ephod.

15 So David and all the house of Israel were bringing up the ark of the LORD with shouting and the **sound** of the **trumpet**.

16 Then it happened *as* the ark of the LORD came into the city of David that Michal the daughter of Saul looked out of the window and saw King David leaping and **dancing** before the LORD; and she despised him in her heart.

ABSALOM'S TREASON

15:1–12

10 But Absalom sent spies throughout all the tribes of

Israel, saying, "As soon as you hear the **sound** of the **trumpet**, then you shall say, 'Absalom is king in Hebron.'"

ABSALOM KILLED

18:9–18

16 Then **Joab blew** the **trumpet**, and the people returned from pursuing Israel, for Joab restrained the people.

DAVID AND BARZILLAI

19:31–39

35 "I am now eighty years old. Can I distinguish between good and bad? Or can your servant taste what I eat or what I drink? Or can I hear anymore the voice of **singing** men and women? Why then should your servant be an added burden to my lord the king?

SHEBA'S TREASON

20:1–22

1 Now a worthless fellow happened to be there whose name was **Sheba**, the son of Bichri, a Benjamite; and he **blew** the **trumpet** and said,

"We have no portion in **David**,
Nor do we have inheritance in the son of Jesse;
Every man to his tents, O Israel!"

22 Then the woman wisely came to all the people. And they cut off the head of Sheba the son of Bichri and threw it to **Joab**. So he **blew** the **trumpet**, and they were dispersed from the city, each to his tent. **Joab** also returned to the king at Jerusalem.

DAVID'S VICTORY SONG

22:1–51

1 And David spoke the words of this **song** to the LORD in the day that the LORD delivered him from the hand of all his enemies and from the hand of Saul.

50 "Therefore I will give thanks to Thee, O LORD, among the nations,
And I will **sing** praises to Thy name.

DAVID'S LAST SONG

23:1–7

1 Now these are the last words of David.

(13

> David the son of Jesse declares,
> And the man who was raised on high declares,
> The anointed of the God of Jacob,
> And the **sweet psalmist** of Israel,

FIRST KINGS

SOLOMON'S CORONATION

1:32–48

34 "And let Zadok the priest and Nathan the prophet anoint him there as king over Israel, and **blow** the **trumpet** and say, '*Long* live King Solomon!'

39 Zadok the priest then took the horn of oil from the tent and anointed Solomon. Then they **blew** the **trumpet**, and all the people said, "*Long* live King Solomon!"

40 And all the people went up after him, and the people were **playing** on **flutes** and rejoicing with great joy, so that the earth shook at their noise.

41 Now Adonijah and all the guests who were with him heard *it*, as they finished eating. When Joab heard the **sound** of the **trumpet**, he said, "Why is the city making such an uproar?"

SOLOMON'S WISDOM

4:29–34

31 For he was wiser than all men, than **Ethan** the Ezrahite, **Heman**, Calcol and Darda, the sons of Mahol; and his fame was *known* in all the surrounding nations.

32 He also spoke 3,000 proverbs, and his **songs** were 1,005.

INSTRUMENTS OF ALMUG TREES

10:11, 12

12 And the king made of the almug trees supports for the house of the LORD and for the king's house, also **lyres** and **harps** for the **singers**; such almug trees have not come in *again*, nor have they been seen to this day.

SECOND KINGS

ELISHA PROPHESIES

3:13–20

15 "But now bring me a **minstrel**." And it came about, when the **minstrel played**, that the hand of the LORD came upon him.

JEHU ANNOINTED

9:11–13

13 Then they hurried and each man took his garment and placed it under him on the bare steps, and **blew** the **trumpet**, saying, "Jehu is king!"

ATHALIAH KILLED

11:13–16

14 And she looked and behold, the king was standing by the pillar, according to the custom, with the captains and the **trumpeters** beside the king; and all the people of the land rejoiced and **blew trumpets**. Then Athaliah tore her clothes and cried, "Treason! Treason!"

COLLECTION FOR TEMPLE REPAIR

12:9–16

13 But there were not made for the house of the LORD silver cups, snuffers, bowls, **trumpets**, any vessels of gold, or vessels of silver from the money which was brought into the house of the LORD;

FIRST CHRONICLES

LEVITE MUSICIANS

6:31–48

31 Now these are those whom **David** appointed over the service of **song** in the house of the LORD, after the ark rested *there*.

32 And they ministered with **song** before the tabernacle of the tent of meeting, until Solomon had built the house of the LORD in Jerusalem; and they served in their office according to their order.

33 And these are those who served with their sons. From the sons of the Kohathites *were* **Heman** the **singer**, the son of Joel, the son of Samuel,

39 And *Heman's* brother **Asaph** stood at his right hand, even **Asaph** the son of Berechiah, the son of Shimea,

44 And on the left hand *were* their kinsmen the sons of Merari: **Ethan** the son of Kishi, the son of Abdi, the son of Malluch,

LEVITE MUSICIANS

9:33–34

33 Now these are the **singers**, heads of fathers' *households* of the Levites, *who lived* in the chambers *of the temple* free *from other service;* for they were engaged in their work day and night.

DAVID MOVES THE ARK

13:1–14

8 And **David** and all Israel were celebrating before God with all *their* might, even with **songs** and with **lyres, harps, tambourines, cymbals,** and with **trumpets**.

LEVITE MUSICIANS

15:16–29

16 Then David spoke to the chiefs of the Levites to appoint their relatives the **singers**, with **instruments** of **music, harps, lyres, loud-sounding cymbal**s, to raise **sounds** of joy.

19 So the **singers, Heman, Asaph,** and **Ethan** *were appointed* to **sound** aloud **cymbals** of bronze;
20 and **Zechariah, Aziel, Shemiramoth, Jehiel, Unni, Eliab, Maaseiah,** and **Benaiah**, with **harps** *tuned* to **alamoth;**
21 and **Mattithiah, Eliphelehu, Mikneiah, Obed-edom, Jeiel,** and **Azaziah**, to lead with **lyres** tuned to the **sheminith.**
22 And **Chenaniah**, chief of the Levites, was *in charge of* the **singing**; he gave instruction in **singing** because he was **skillful**.

24 And **Shebaniah, Joshaphat, Nethanel, Amasa**i, **Zechariah, Benaiah,** and **Eliezer**, the priests, **blew** the **trumpets** before the ark of God. Obed-edom and Jehiah also *were* gatekeepers for the ark.

27 Now **David** was clothed with a robe of fine linen with all the Levites who were carrying the ark, and the

singers and **Chenaniah** the leader of the **singing** *with* the singers. David also wore an ephod of linen.

28 Thus all Israel brought up the ark of the covenant of the LORD with shouting, and with **sound** of the **horn**, with **trumpets**, with loud-sounding **cymbals**, with **harp**s and **lyres**.

LEVITE MUSICIANS AND THEIR SONG

16:1–43

4 And he appointed some of the Levites *as* ministers before the ark of the LORD, even to celebrate and to thank and praise the LORD God of Israel:

5 **Asaph** the chief, and second to him **Zechariah**, *then* **Jeiel, Shemiramoth, Jehiel, Mattithiah, Eliab, Benaiah, Obed-edom**, and **Jeiel**, with **musical instruments, harps, lyres**; also **Asaph** *played* **loud-sounding cymbals**,

6 and **Benaiah** and **Jahaziel** the priests *blew* **trumpets** continually before the ark of the covenant of God.

9 **Sing** to Him, **sing** praises to Him; Speak of all His wonders.

33 Then the trees of the forest will **sing** for joy before the LORD; For He is coming to judge the earth.

42 And with them *were* **Heman** and **Jeduthun** *with* **trumpets** and **cymbals** for those who should **sound** aloud, and *with* **instruments** *for* the **songs** of God, and the sons of **Jeduthun** for the gate.

LEVITE MUSICIANS

23:1–6

5 and 4,000 *were* gatekeepers, and 4,000 *were* praising the LORD with the **instruments** which **David** made for giving praise.

25:1–31

1 Moreover, David and the commanders of the army set apart for the service *some* of the sons of **Asaph** and of **Heman** and of **Jeduthun**, who *were* to prophesy with **lyres, harps**, and **cymbals**; and the number of those who performed their service was:

2 Of the sons of **Asaph**: **Zaccur, Joseph, Nethaniah**, and **Asharelah**; the sons of **Asaph** *were* under the direction of **Asaph**, who prophesied under the direction of the king.

(17

3 Of **Jeduthun,** the sons of **Jeduthun: Gedaliah, Zeri, Jeshaiah, Shimei, Hashabiah,** and **Mattithiah,** six, under the direction of their father **Jeduthun** with the **harp,** who prophesied in giving thanks and praising the LORD.

4 Of **Heman,** the sons of **Heman: Bukkiah, Mattaniah, Uzziel, Shebuel** and **Jerimoth, Hananiah, Hanani, Eliathah, Giddalti** and **Romamti-ezer, Joshbekashah, Mallothi, Hothir, Mahazioth.**

5 All these *were* the sons of **Heman** the king's seer to exalt him according to the words of God, for God gave fourteen sons and three daughters to **Heman.**

6 All these were under the direction of their father to **sing** in the house of the LORD, with **cymbals, harps** and **lyres,** for the service of the house of God. **Asaph, Jeduthun** and **Heman** *were* under the direction of the king.

7 And their number who were trained in **singing** to the LORD, with their relatives, all who were **skillful,** *was* 288.

SECOND CHRONICLES

TEMPLE DEDICATION

5:11–14

12 and all the Levitical singers, **Asaph, Heman, Jeduthun,** and their sons and kinsmen, clothed in fine linen, with **cymbals, harps,** and **lyres,** standing east of the altar, and with them one hundred and twenty priests **blowing trumpets**

13 in **unison** when the **trumpeters** and the **singers** were to make themselves heard with one voice to praise and to glorify the LORD, and when they lifted up their voice **accompanied** by **trumpets** and **cymbals** and **instruments** of **music,** and when they praised the LORD *saying,* "He indeed is good for His lovingkindness is everlasting," then the house, the house of the LORD, was filled with a cloud,

SOLOMON'S SACRIFICES

7:4–7

6 And the priests stood at their posts and the Levites, with the **instruments** of **music** to the LORD, which King David had made for giving praise to the LORD— "for His

lovingkindness is everlasting"— whenever he gave praise by their means, while the priests on the other side **blew trumpets**; and all Israel was standing.

SOLOMON AND THE QUEEN OF SHEBA

9:1–12   11 And from the algum the king made steps for the house of the LORD and for the king's palace, and **lyres** and **harps** for the **singers**; and none like that was seen before in the land of Judah.

ABIJAH EXHORTS ISRAEL

13:4–12   12 "Now behold, God is with us at *our* head and His priests with the **signal trumpets** to sound the alarm against you. O sons of Israel, do not fight against the LORD God of your fathers, for you will not succeed."

ISRAEL AND JUDAH AT WAR

13:13–20   14 When Judah turned around, behold, they were attacked both front and rear; so they cried to the LORD, and the priests **blew** the **trumpets**.

ASA REMOVES IDOLS

15:8–15   14 Moreover, they made an oath to the LORD with a loud voice, with shouting, with **trumpets**, and with **horns**.

JEHOSHAPHAT AT WAR

20:20–30   21 And when he had consulted with the people, he appointed those who **sang** to the LORD and those who praised *Him* in holy attire, as they went out before the army and said, "Give thanks to the LORD, for His lovingkindness is everlasting."

22 And when they began **singing** and praising, the LORD set ambushes against the sons of Ammon, Moab, and Mount Seir, who had come against Judah; so they were routed.

28 And they came to Jerusalem with **harps**, **lyres**, and **trumpets** to the house of the LORD.

ATHALIAH KILLED

23:12–15   13 And she looked, and behold, the king was standing by his pillar at the entrance, and the captains and the **trumpeters** *were* beside the king. And all the people of the land rejoiced and **blew trumpets**, the **singers** with *their* **musical instruments** leading the praise. Then Athaliah tore her clothes and said, "Treason! Treason!"

JEHOIDA RENOUNCES BAAL

23:16–21

18 Moreover, Jehoiada placed the offices of the house of the LORD under the authority of the Levitical priests, whom David had assigned over the house of the LORD, to offer the burnt offerings of the LORD, as it is written in the law of Moses—with rejoicing and **singing** according to the order of David.

HEZEKIAH SACRIFICES AND WORSHIPS

29:20–36

25 He then stationed the Levites in the house of the LORD with **cymbals**, with **harps**, and with **lyres**, according to the command of David and of Gad the king's seer, and of Nathan the prophet; for the command was from the LORD through His prophets.

26 And the Levites stood with the *musical* **instruments** of David, and the priests with the **trumpets**.

27 Then Hezekiah gave the order to offer the burnt offering on the altar. When the burnt offering began, the **song** to the LORD also began with the **trumpets**, *accompanied* by the **instruments** of David, king of Israel.

28 While the whole assembly worshiped, the **singers** also **sang** and the **trumpets sounded**; all this *continued* until the burnt offering was finished.

30 Moreover, King Hezekiah and the officials ordered the Levites to **sing** praises to the LORD with the words of David and Asaph the seer. So they **sang** praises with joy, and bowed down and worshiped.

FEAST OF UNLEAVENED BREAD

30:13–22

21 And the sons of Israel present in Jerusalem celebrated the Feast of Unleavened Bread *for* seven days with great joy, and the Levites and the priests praised the LORD day after day with loud **instruments** to the LORD.

TEMPLE REPAIR

34:8–13

12 And the men did the work faithfully with foremen over them to supervise: **Jahath** and **Obadiah**, the **Levites** of the sons of **Merari**, **Zechariah** and **Meshullam** of the sons of the **Kohathites**, and the Levites, all who were **skillful** with **musical instruments**.

THE PASSOVER

35:10–15

15 The **singers**, the sons of **Asaph**, *were* also at their stations according to the command of **David**, **Asaph**, **Heman**, and **Jeduthun** the king's seer; and the gatekeepers at each gate did not have to depart from their service, because the Levites their brethren prepared for them.

LAMENT FOR JOSIAH

35:20–27

25 Then **Jeremiah chanted** a **lament** for **Josiah**. And all the male and female **singers** speak about Josiah in their lamentations to this day. And they made them an ordinance in Israel; behold, they are also written in the Lamentations.

EZRA

RETURN FROM EXILE

2:1–70

41 The **singers**: the sons of **Asaph**, 128.

65 besides their male and female servants, who numbered 7,337; and they had 200 **singing** men and women.

70 Now the priests and the Levites, some of the people, the **singers**, the gatekeepers, and the temple servants lived in their cities, and all Israel in their cities.

REJOICING OVER TEMPLE REBUILDING

3:8–13

10 Now when the builders had laid the foundation of the temple of the LORD, the priests stood in their apparel with **trumpets**, and the Levites, the sons of **Asaph**, with **cymbals**, to praise the LORD according to the directions of

King David of Israel.

11 And they **sang**, praising and giving thanks to the LORD, *saying,* "For He is good, for His lovingkindness is upon Israel forever." And all the people shouted with a great shout when they praised the LORD because the foundation of the house of the LORD was laid.

EZRA AND EXILES RETURN

7:1–10   7 And some of the sons of Israel and some of the priests, the Levites, the **singers**, the gatekeepers, and the temple servants went up to Jerusalem in the seventh year of King Artaxerxes.

TAX LAWS

7:11–26   24 "We also inform you that it is not allowed to impose tax, tribute or toll *on* any of the priests, Levites, **singers**, doorkeepers, Nethinim, or servants of this house of God.

MARRIAGE TO FOREIGN WOMEN

10:18–24   **24** And of the **singers** *there was* **Eliashib**; and of the gatekeepers: Shallum, Telem, and Uri.

NEHEMIAH

REBUILDING OF THE WALL

4:15–23   18 As for the builders, each *wore* his sword girded at his side as he built, while the **trumpeter** *stood* near me.

20 "At whatever place you hear the **sound** of the **trumpet**, rally to us there. Our God will fight for us."

APPOINTED SINGERS

7:1–2   1 Now it came about when the wall was rebuilt and I had set up the doors, and the gatekeepers and the **singers** and the Levites were appointed,

RETURNEES FROM EXILE

7:5–73   44 The **singers**: the sons of **Asaph**, 148.

67 besides their male and their female servants, of whom *there were* 7,337; and they had 245 male and female **singers**.

73 Now the priests, the Levites, the gatekeepers, the **singers**, some of the people, the temple servants, and all Israel, lived in their cities.

DEDICATION TO GOD'S SERVICE

10:28–31   **28** Now the rest of the people, the priests, the Levites, the gatekeepers, the **singers**, the temple servants, and all those who had separated themselves from the peoples of the lands to the law of God, their wives, their sons and their daughters, all those who had knowledge and understanding,

SUPPORT FOR THE LEVITES

10:34–39   39 For the sons of Israel and the sons of Levi shall bring the contribution of the grain, the new wine and the oil, to the chambers; there are the utensils of the sanctuary, the priests who are ministering, the gatekeepers, and the **singers**. Thus we will not neglect the house of our God.

LEVITE OVERSEERS

11:22–24   **22** Now the overseer of the Levites in Jerusalem was Uzzi the son of Bani, the son of Hashabiah, the son of Mattaniah, the son of Mica, from the sons of **Asaph**, who were the **singers** for the service of the house of God.

23 For *there was* a commandment from the king concerning them and a firm regulation for the **song leaders** day by day.

DEDICATION OF THE WALL

12:27–47   **27** Now at the dedication of the wall of Jerusalem they sought out the Levites from all their places, to bring them to Jerusalem so that they might celebrate the dedication with gladness, with **hymns** of thanksgiving and with **songs** *to the accompaniment* of **cymbals**, **harps**, and **lyres**.

28 So the sons of the **singers** were assembled from the district around Jerusalem, and from the villages of the Netophathites,

29 from Beth-gilgal, and from *their* fields in Geba and Azmaveth, for the **singers** had built themselves villages around Jerusalem.

31 Then I had the leaders of Judah come up on top of the wall, and I appointed two great **choirs**, the first proceeding to the right on top of the wall toward the Refuse Gate.

35 and some of the sons of the priests with **trumpets**; *and* Zechariah the son of Jonathan, the son of Shemaiah, the son of Mattaniah, the son of Micaiah, the son of Zaccur, the son of **Asaph**,

36 and his kinsmen, **Shemaiah, Azarel, Milalai, Gilalai, Maai, Nethanel, Judah** *and* **Hanani**, with the **musical instruments** of **David** the man of God. And Ezra the scribe went before them.

38 The second **choir** proceeded to the left, while I followed them with half of the people on the wall, above the Tower of Furnaces, to the Broad Wall,

40 Then the two **choirs** took their stand in the house of God. So did I and half of the officials with me;

41 and the priests, **Eliakim, Maaseiah, Miniamin, Micaiah, Elioenai, Zechariah**, and **Hananiah**, with the **trumpets**;

42 and **Maaseiah, Shemaiah, Eleazar, Uzzi, Jehohanan, Malchijah, Elam**, and **Ezer**. And the **singers** sang, with **Jezrahiah** *their* leader,

45 For they performed the worship of their God and the service of purification, together with the **singers** and the gatekeepers in accordance with the command of **David** *and* of his son **Solomon**.

46 For in the days of **David** and **Asaph**, in ancient times, *there were* leaders of the **singers, songs** of praise and **hymns** of thanksgiving to God.

47 And so all Israel in the days of Zerubbabel and Nehemiah gave the portions due the **singers** and the gatekeepers as each day required, and set apart the consecrated *portion* for the Levites, and the Levites set apart the consecrated *portion* for the sons of Aaron.

SUPPORT NEGLECTED

13:4–14

5 had prepared a large room for him, where formerly they put the grain offerings, the frankincense, the utensils, and the tithes of grain, wine and oil prescribed for the Levites, the **singers** and the gatekeepers, and the contributions for the priests.

10 I also discovered that the portions of the Levites had not been given *them*, so that the Levites and the **singers** who performed the service had gone away, each to his own field.

ESTHER

JOB

THE PROSPERITY OF THE WICKED

21:1–16

12 "They **sing** to the **timbrel** and **harp**
And rejoice at the **sound** of the **flute**.

JOB DESIRES PAST GLORY

29:1–25

13 "The blessing of the one ready to perish
came upon me,
And I made the widow's heart **sing** for joy.

REASONS FOR SORROW

30:24–31

31 "Therefore my **harp** is turned to mourning,
And my **flute** to the sound of those who
weep.

THE WORK OF AN ANGEL

33:23–28

27 "He will **sing** to men and say,
'I have sinned and perverted what is right,
And it is not proper for me.

MAN'S CRIES TO GOD

35:9–16

10 "But no one says, 'Where is God my Maker,
Who gives **songs** in the night,

(25

GOD'S MAGNIFICENCE

| 36:24–33 | **24** | "Remember that you should exalt His work,
Of which men have **sung**. |

GOD QUESTIONS JOB

| 38:1–7 | 7 | When the morning stars **sang** together,
And all the sons of God shouted for joy? |

GOD QUESTIONS JOB

| 39:19–25 | 24 | "With shaking and rage he races over the ground;
And he does not stand still at the voice of the **trumpet**. |
| | 25 | "As often as the **trumpet** *sounds* he says, 'Aha!'
And he scents the battle from afar,
And thunder of the captains, and the war cry. |

THE PSALMS

Note: The psalms are poetry contributions from various authors and form the hymn book of biblical times. As such, each psalm is a potential song text.

The superscription of each psalm was included as part of the psalm in the original text. Because of this, and because of the insights they provide, they are included in this compilation.

The term selah *is considered a musical term by most authorities and is therefore included as such.*

SUPERSCRIPTION

| 3:0 | A **Psalm** of **David**, when he fled from Absalom his son. |

SELAH

3:2, 4, 8

SUPERSCRIPTION

| 4:0 | For the **choir director**; on **stringed instruments**. A **Psalm** of **David**. |

SELAH

4:2, 4

SUPERSCRIPTION

5:0   For the **choir director**; for **flute accompaniment**. A **Psalm** of **David**.

SUPERSCRIPTION

6:0   For the **choir director**; with **stringed instruments**, upon an **eight-stringed lyre**. A **Psalm** of **David**.

SUPERSCRIPTION

7:0   A **Shiggaion** of **David**, which he **sang** to the LORD concerning Cush, a Benjamite.

SELAH

7:5

PRAISE AND THANKSGIVING

7:17   **17** I will give thanks to the LORD according to His righteousness,
And will **sing** praise to the name of the LORD Most High.

SUPERSCRIPTION

8:0   For the **choir director**; on the **Gittith**. A **Psalm** of **David**.

SUPERSCRIPTION

9:0   For the **choir director**; on **Muth-labben**. A **Psalm** of **David**.

PRAISE AND THANKSGIVING

9:1, 2   2 I will be glad and exult in Thee;
I will **sing** praise to Thy name, O Most High.

PRAISE

9:11–16   **11**   **Sing** praises to the LORD, who dwells in Zion;
Declare among the peoples His deeds.

SELAH

9:16, 20

SUPERSCRIPTION

11:0   For the **choir director**. *A Psalm* of **David**.

SUPERSCRIPTION

12:0   For the **choir director**; upon an **eight-stringed lyre**. A **Psalm** of **David**.

SUPERSCRIPTION

13:0   For the **choir director**. A **Psalm** of **David**.

PRAISE

13:5, 6   6   I will **sing** to the LORD,
                         Because He has dealt bountifully with me.

SUPERSCRIPTION

14:0   For the **choir director**. *A Psalm* of **David**.

SUPERSCRIPTION

15:0   A **Psalm** of **David**.

SUPERSCRIPTION

16:0   A **Mikhtam** of **David**.

SUPERSCRIPTION

17:0   A Prayer of **David**.

SUPERSCRIPTION

18:0   For the **choir director**. *A Psalm* of **David** the servant of the LORD, who spoke to the LORD the words of this **song** in the day that the LORD delivered him from the hand of all his enemies and from the hand of Saul. And he said,)

PRAISE AND THANKSGIVING

18:46–50   49   Therefore I will give thanks to Thee among the nations, O LORD,
                         And I will **sing** praises to Thy name.

SUPERSCRIPTION

19:0

For the **choir director**. A **Psalm** of **David**.

SUPERSCRIPTION

20:0

For the **choir director**. A **Psalm** of **David**.

SELAH

20:3

SUPERSCRIPTION

21:0

For the **choir director**. A **Psalm** of **David**.

SELAH

21:2

PRAISE

21:7–13

13　Be Thou exalted, O LORD, in Thy strength;
We will **sing** and praise Thy power.

SUPERSCRIPTION

22:0

For the **choir director**; upon **Aijeleth Hashshahar**. A **Psalm** of **David**.

SUPERSCRIPTION

23:0

A **Psalm** of **David**.

SUPERSCRIPTION

24:0

A **Psalm** of **David**.

SELAH

24:6, 10

SUPERSCRIPTION

25:0

A Psalm of **David**.

SUPERSCRIPTION

26:0

A Psalm of **David**.

SUPERSCRIPTION

27:0

A Psalm of **David**.

TEMPLE WORSHIP

27:4–6

6 And now my head will be lifted up above my
enemies around me;
And I will offer in His tent sacrifices with
shouts of joy;
I will **sing**, yes, I will **sing** praises to the
LORD.

SUPERSCRIPTION

28:0

*A **Psalm** of **David**.*

THANKSGIVING

28:6–9

7 The LORD is my strength and my shield;
My heart trusts in Him, and I am helped;
Therefore my heart exults,
And with my **song** I shall thank Him.

SUPERSCRIPTION

29:0

A **Psalm** of **David**.

SUPERSCRIPTION

30:0

A **Psalm**; a **Song** at the Dedication of the House. *A **Psalm***
of **David**.

PRAISE AND THANKSGIVING

30:1–5

4 **Sing** praise to the LORD, you His godly ones,
And give thanks to His holy name.

30:10–12

11 Thou hast turned for me my mourning into
dancing;
Thou hast loosed my sackcloth and girded
me with gladness;
12 That *my* soul may **sing** praise to Thee, and
not be silent.
O LORD my God, I will give thanks to Thee
forever.

SUPERSCRIPTION

31:0

For the **choir director**. A **Psalm** of **David**.

32:0   *A **Psalm** of **David**. A **Maskil**.*

CONFESSION OF SIN

32:3–7   7   Thou art my hiding place;
                    Thou dost preserve me from trouble;
                    Thou dost surround me with **songs** of
                        deliverance.

PRAISE AND THANKSGIVING

33:1–5   1   **Sing** for joy in the LORD, O you righteous
                        ones;
                    Praise is becoming to the upright.
                2   Give thanks to the LORD with the **lyre**;
                    Sing praises to Him with a **harp** of **ten
                        strings**.
                3   **Sing** to Him a new **song**;
                    Play skillfully with a shout of joy.

SUPERSCRIPTION

34:0   *A **Psalm** of **David*** when he feigned madness before
                        Abimelech, who drove him away and he departed.

SUPERSCRIPTION

35:0   *A **Psalm** of **David**.*

SUPERSCRIPTION

36:0   For the **choir director**. *A **Psalm** of **David*** the servant of
                        the LORD.

SUPERSCRIPTION

37:0   A **Psalm** of **David**.

SUPERSCRIPTION

38:0   A **Psalm** of **David**, for a memorial.

SUPERSCRIPTION

39:0   For the **choir director**, for **Jeduthun**. A **Psalm** of **David**.

SELAH

39:5, 11

SUPERSCRIPTION

40:0   For the **choir director**. A **Psalm** of **David**.

PRAISE FOR DELIVERANCE

40:1–3   3   And He put a new **song** in my mouth, a **song**
                            of praise to our God;
                    Many will see and fear,
                    And will trust in the LORD.

SUPERSCRIPTION

41:0   For the **choir director**. A **Psalm** of **David**.

SUPERSCRIPTION

42:0   For the **choir director**. A **Maskil** of the sons of **Korah**.

GOD'S PRESENCE IN DESPAIR

42:5–8   8   The LORD will command His lovingkindness
                    in the daytime;
                    And His **song** will be with me in the night,
                    A prayer to the God of my life.

PRAISE AND OFFERINGS

43:1–4   4   Then I will go to the altar of God,
                    To God my exceeding joy;
                    And upon the **lyre** I shall praise Thee, O
                    God, my God.

SUPERSCRIPTION

44:0   For the **choir director**. A **Maskil** of the sons of **Korah**.

SELAH

44:8

SUPERSCRIPTION

45:0   For the **choir director**; according to the **Shoshannim**. A
                 Maskil of the sons of **Korah**. A **Song** of Love.

SUPERSCRIPTION

46:0   For the **choir director**. *A Psalm* of the sons of **Korah**, set
               to **Alamoth**. A **Song**.

SELAH

46: 3, 7, 11

SUPERSCRIPTION

47:0   For the **choir director**. A **Psalm** of the sons of **Korah**.

SELAH

47:4

PRAISE

47:5–9   **5**   God has ascended with a shout,
                   The LORD, with the **sound** of a **trumpet**.
          6   **Sing** praises to God, **sing** praises;
                   Sing praises to our King, **sing** praises.
          7   For God is the King of all the earth;
                   Sing praises with a **skillful psalm**.

SUPERSCRIPTION

48:0   A **Song**; a **Psalm** of the sons of **Korah**.

SELAH

48:8

SUPERSCRIPTION

49:0   For the **choir director**. A **Psalm** of the sons of **Korah**.

A WITNESS TO ALL PEOPLES

49:1–4   4   I will incline my ear to a proverb;
                   I will express my riddle on the **harp**.

SELAH

49:13, 15

SUPERSCRIPTION

50:0   A **Psalm** of **Asaph**.

SELAH

50:6

SUPERSCRIPTION

51:0   For the **choir director**. A **Psalm** of **David**, when Nathan the prophet came to him, after he had gone in to Bathsheba.

SACRIFICES AND FORGIVENESS

51:14–17 **14** Deliver me from bloodguiltiness, O God,
        Thou God of my salvation;
        Then my tongue will joyfully **sing** of Thy
        righteousness.

SUPERSCRIPTION

52:0   For the **choir director**. A **Maskil** of **David**, when Doeg the Edomite came and told Saul, and said to him, "David has come to the house of Ahimelech."

SELAH

52:3, 5

SUPERSCRIPTION

53:0   For the **choir director**; according to **Mahalath**. A **Maskil** of **David**.

SUPERSCRIPTION

54:0   For the **choir director**; on **stringed instruments**. A **Maskil** of **David**, when the Ziphites came and said to Saul, "Is not David hiding himself among us?"

SELAH

54:3

SUPERSCRIPTION

55:0   For the **choir director**; on **stringed instruments**. A **Maskil** of **David**.

SELAH

55:7, 19

SUPERSCRIPTION

56:0   For the **choir director**; according to **Jonath elem rehokim**. A **Mikhtam** of **David**, when the Philistines seized him in Gath.

SUPERSCRIPTION

57:0   For the **choir director**; *set to* **Al-tashheth**. A **Mikhtam** of **David**, when he fled from Saul, in the cave.

SELAH

57:3, 6

PRAISE AND THANKSGIVING

57:7–11   **7** My heart is steadfast, O God, my heart is steadfast;
                  I will **sing**, yes, I will **sing** praises!
      8 Awake, my glory;
                  Awake, **harp** and **lyre**,
                  I will awaken the dawn!
      9 I will give thanks to Thee, O Lord, among the peoples;
                  I will **sing** praises to Thee among the nations.

SUPERSCRIPTION

58:0   For the **choir director**; *set to* **Al-tashheth**. A **Mikhtam** of **David**.

SUPERSCRIPTION

59:0   For the **choir director**; *set to* **Al-tashheth**. A **Mikhtam** of **David**, when Saul sent *men,* and they watched the house in order to kill him.

SELAH

59:5, 13

PRAISE

59:16, 17   **16** But as for me, I shall **sing** of Thy strength;
                    Yes, I shall joyfully **sing** of Thy lovingkindness in the morning,

> For Thou hast been my stronghold,
> And a refuge in the day of my distress.
> 17   O my strength, I will **sing** praises to Thee;
> For God is my stronghold, the God who
> shows me lovingkindness.

SUPERSCRIPTION

60:0   For the **choir director**; according to **Shushan Eduth**. A **Mikhtam** of **David**, to teach; when he struggled with Aram-naharaim and with Aram-zobah, and Joab returned, and smote twelve thousand of Edom in the Valley of Salt.

SELAH

60:4

SUPERSCRIPTION

61:0   For the **choir director**; on a **stringed instrument**. *A Psalm* of **David**.

SELAH

61:4

PRAISE FOR THE KING'S LONGEVITY

61:5–8   8   So I will **sing** praise to Thy name forever,
That I may pay my vows day by day.

SUPERSCRIPTION

62:0   For the **choir director**; according to **Jeduthun**. A **Psalm** of **David**.

SELAH

62:4, 8

SUPERSCRIPTION

63:0   A **Psalm** of **David**, when he was in the wilderness of Judah.

SUPERSCRIPTION

64:0   For the **choir director**. A **Psalm** of **David**.

65:0   For the **choir director**. A **Psalm** of **David**. A **Song**.

GOD IN NATURE

65:9–13   13   The meadows are clothed with flocks,
                                And the valleys are covered with grain;
                                They shout for joy, yes, they **sing**.

SUPERSCRIPTION

66:0   For the **choir director**. A **Song**. A **Psalm**.

PRAISE FOR GOD'S GREATNESS

66:1–4   2   **Sing** the glory of His name;
                                Make His praise glorious.

                  4   "All the earth will worship Thee,
                                And will **sing** praises to Thee;
                                They will **sing** praises to Thy name."

SELAH

66:4, 7, 15

SUPERSCRIPTION

67:0   For the **choir director**; with **stringed instruments**. A **Psalm**. A **Song**.

SELAH

67:1, 4

PRAISE

67:1–7   4   Let the nations be glad and **sing** for joy;
                                For Thou wilt judge the peoples with up-
                                      rightness,
                                And guide the nations on the earth.

SUPERSCRIPTION

68:0   For the **choir director**. A **Psalm** of **David**. A **Song**.

PRAISE

68:1–4   4   **Sing** to God, **sing** praises to His name; Cast up a

highway for him who rides through the deserts,
Whose name is the LORD, and exult before Him.

SELAH

68:7, 19, 32

TEMPLE WORSHIP

68:24–27   25   The **singers** went on, the **musicians** after
them,
In the midst of the maidens beating **tambourines**.

GOD'S MAJESTY

68:32–35   **32** **Sing** to God, O kingdoms of the earth;
Sing praises to the Lord,

SUPERSCRIPTION

69:0   For the **choir director**; according to **Shoshannim**. *A
Psalm* of **David**.

DERISION BY ENEMIES

69:5–12   12   Those who sit in the gate talk about me,
And I *am* the **song** of the drunkards.

RESOLUTION TO PRAISE

69:29–33   30   I will praise the name of God with **song**,
And shall magnify Him with thanksgiving.

SUPERSCRIPTION

70:0   For the **choir director**. *A Psalm* of **David**; for a memorial.

PRAISE TO GOD

71:22–24   **22** I will also praise Thee with a **harp**,
Even Thy truth, O my God;
To Thee I will **sing** praises with the **lyre**,
O Thou Holy One of Israel.
23   My lips will shout for joy when I **sing** praises
to Thee;
And my soul, which Thou hast redeemed.

78:0   A **Maskil** of **Asaph.**

79:0   A **Psalm** of **Asaph.**

80:0   For the **choir director**; *set to* **El Shoshannim**; **Eduth.** A **Psalm** of **Asaph.**

81:0   (For the **choir director**; on the **Gittith.** *A Psalm* of **Asaph.**)

81:1–5
1   **Sing** for joy to God our strength;
Shout joyfully to the God of Jacob.
2   Raise a **song**, **strike** the **timbrel**,
The **sweet sounding lyre** with the **harp**
3   **Blow** the **trumpet** at the new moon,
At the full moon, on our feast day.

81:7

82:0   A **Psalm** of **Asaph.**

82:2

83:0   A **Song**, a **Psalm** of **Asaph.**

83:8

84:0   For the **choir director**; on the **Gittith.** A **Psalm** of the sons of **Korah.**

SELAH

84:4, 8

SUPERSCRIPTION

85:0   For the **choir director**. A **Psalm** of the sons of **Korah**.

SELAH

85:2

SUPERSCRIPTION

86:0   A **Prayer** of **David**.

SUPERSCRIPTION

87:0   A **Psalm** of the sons of **Korah**. A **Song**.

SELAH

87:3, 6

PRAISE TO JERUSALEM

87:1–7   7   Then those who **sing** as well as those who
                   play the **flutes** *shall say*,
                   "All my springs *of joy* are in you."

SUPERSCRIPTION

88:0   A **Song**. A **Psalm** of the sons of **Korah**. For the **choir
              director**; according to **Mahalath Leannoth**. A **Maskil** of
              Heman the Ezrahite.

SELAH

88:7, 10

SUPERSCRIPTION

89:0   A **Maskil** of **Ethan** the Ezrahite.

GOD'S FAITHFULNESS

89:1–4   1   I will **sing** of the lovingkindness of the LORD
                   forever;
                   To all generations I will make known Thy
                   faithfulness with my mouth.

Psalms

SELAH

89:4, 37, 45, 48

SUPERSCRIPTION

90:0   A Prayer of **Moses** the man of God.

SUPERSCRIPTION

92:0   A **Psalm**, a **Song** for the Sabbath day.

PRAISE AND THANKSGIVING

92:1–4   1   It is good to give thanks to the LORD,
                   And to **sing** praises to Thy name, O Most
                   High;

              3   With the **ten-stringed lute**, and with the
                   harp;
                   With **resounding music** upon the **lyre**.
              4   For Thou, O LORD, hast made me glad by
                   what Thou hast done,
                   I will **sing** for joy at the works of Thy hands.

PRAISE

95:1–5   1   O come, let us **sing** for joy to the LORD;
                   Let us shout joyfully to the rock of our salva-
                   tion.
              2   Let us come before His presence with
                   thanksgiving;
                   Let us shout joyfully to Him with **psalms**.

PRAISE WITH A NEW SONG

96:1–6   1   **Sing** to the LORD a new song;
                   Sing to the LORD, all the earth.
              2   **Sing** to the LORD, bless His name;
                   Proclaim good tidings of His salvation from
                   day to day.

SUPERSCRIPTION

98:0   A **Psalm.**

42)

PRAISE

98:1–6

1   O **sing** to the LORD a new song,
      For He has done wonderful things,
      His right hand and His holy arm have gained the
          victory for Him.

4   Shout joyfully to the LORD, all the earth;
      Break forth and **sing** for joy and **sing** praises.
5   **Sing** praises to the LORD with the **lyre**;
      With the **lyre** and the **sound** of **melody**.
6   With **trumpets** and the **sound** of the **horn**
      Shout joyfully before the King, the LORD.

SUPERSCRIPTION

100:0   A **Psalm** for Thanksgiving.

PRAISE TO CREATOR

100:1–3

2   Serve the LORD with gladness;
      Come before Him with joyful **singing**.

SUPERSCRIPTION

101:0   A **Psalm** of **David**.

PROFESSION OF UPRIGHTNESS

101:1–5

1   I will **sing** of lovingkindness and justice,
      To Thee, O LORD, I will **sing** praises.

SUPERSCRIPTION

102:0   A Prayer of the Afflicted, when he is faint, and pours out
         his complaint before the LORD.

SUPERSCRIPTION

103:0   *A Psalm* of **David**.

PRAISE

104:31–35

33   I will **sing** to the LORD as long as I live;
      I will **sing** praise to my God while I have my
          being.

PRAISE FOR GOD'S WISDOM

105:1–7   2   **Sing** to Him, **sing** praises to Him;
                  Speak of all His wonders.

RED SEA DELIVERANCE

106:6–12   12   Then they believed His words;
                  They **sang** His praise.

SUPERSCRIPTION

108:0   A **Song**, a **Psalm** of **David**.

PRAISE AND THANKSGIVING

108:1–6   1   My heart is steadfast, O God;
                  I will **sing**, I will **sing** praises, even with my
                  soul.
            2   Awake, **harp** and **lyre**; I will awaken the dawn!
            3   I will give thanks to Thee, O LORD, among
                  the peoples;
                  And I will **sing** praises to Thee among the
                  nations.

SUPERSCRIPTION

109:0   For the **choir director**. A **Psalm** of **David**.

SUPERSCRIPTION

110:0   A **Psalm** of **David**.

SUPERSCRIPTION

117:0   A **Psalm** of Praise

DELIVERANCE FROM THE NATIONS

118:10–14   14   The LORD is my strength and **song**,
                  And He has become my salvation.

THE LORD'S WORD

119:49–56   54   Thy statutes are my **songs**
                  In the house of my pilgrimage.

SUPERSCRIPTION

120:0   A **Song** of **Ascents**.

SUPERSCRIPTION

121:0   A **Song** of **Ascents**.

SUPERSCRIPTION

122:0   A **Song** of **Ascents**, of **David**.

SUPERSCRIPTION

123:0   A **Song** of **Ascents**.

SUPERSCRIPTION

124:0   A **Song** of **Ascents**, of **David**.

SUPERSCRIPTION

125:0   A **Song** of **Ascents**.

SUPERSCRIPTION

126:0   A **Song** of **Ascents**.

SUPERSCRIPTION

127:0   A **Song** of **Ascents**, of **Solomon**.

SUPERSCRIPTION

128:0   A **Song** of **Ascents**.

SUPERSCRIPTION

129:0   A **Song** of **Ascents**.

SUPERSCRIPTION

130:0   A **Song** of **Ascents**.

SUPERSCRIPTION

131:0   A **Song** of **Ascents**, of **David**.

SUPERSCRIPTION

132:0   A **Song** of **Ascents**.

141:0 A **Psalm** of **David**.

142:0 **Maskil** of **David**, when he was in the cave. A Prayer.

143:0 A **Psalm** of **David**.

143:6

144:0 *A **Psalm*** of **David**.

PRAYER FOR RESCUE

144:9–11   9   I will **sing** a new **song** to Thee, O God;
Upon a **harp** of **ten strings** I will **sing** praises
to Thee,

145:0 *A **Psalm*** *of* Praise, of **David**.

PRAISE FOR LIFE

146:1–7   2   I will praise the LORD while I live;
I will **sing** praises to my God while I have my
being.

PRAISE FOR THE LORD'S WORKS

147:1–11   1   Praise the LORD!
For it is good to **sing** praises to our God;
For it is pleasant *and* praise is becoming.

  7   **Sing** to the LORD with thanksgiving;
Sing praises to our God on the **lyre**,

PRAISE

149:1–9   1   Praise the LORD!
Sing to the LORD a new **song**,
And His praise in the congregation of the

godly ones.

3   Let them praise His name with **dancing**;
Let them **sing** praises to Him with **timbrel**
and **lyre**.

5   Let the godly ones exult in glory;
Let them **sing** for joy on their beds.

PRAISE

150:1–6   **3**   Praise Him with **trumpet sound**;
Praise Him with **harp** and **lyre**.

4   Praise Him with **timbrel** and **dancing**;
Praise Him with **stringed instruments** and
pipe.

5   Praise Him with loud **cymbals**;
Praise Him with **resounding cymbals**.

PROVERBS

MUSIC FOR THE TROUBLED

25:20   20   *Like* one who takes off a garment on a cold
day, *or like* vinegar on soda,
Is he who **sings songs** to a troubled heart.

THE RIGHTEOUS SING

29:6   6   By transgression an evil man is ensnared,
But the righteous **sings** and rejoices.

ECCLESIASTES

SOLOMON'S PLEASURES

2:1–11   8 Also, I collected for myself silver and gold, and the
treasure of kings and provinces. I provided for myself male
and female **singers** and the pleasures of men—many con-
cubines.

A TIME FOR EVERYTHING

3:1–8   4   A time to weep, and a time to laugh;

A time to mourn, and a time to **dance**.

REBUKE VERSUS MUSIC

7:1–14   5   It is better to listen to the rebuke of a wise man
                     Than for one to listen to the **song** of fools.

OLD AGE

12:1–8   4   and the doors on the street are shut as the sound of
                     the grinding mill is low, and one will arise at the sound of
                     the bird, and all the daughters of **song** will **sing** softly.

THE SONG OF SOLOMON

Note: This whole book is the text of a song.

1:1   1   The **Song** of **Songs**, which is Solomon's.

ISAIAH

Note: Much of Isaiah is poetry, and as such might have been sung.

A SONG FOR THE BELOVED

5:1–17   1   Let me **sing** now for my well-beloved
                     A **song** of my beloved concerning His vineyard.
                     My well-beloved had a vineyard on a fertile hill.

               12   And their banquets are *accompanied* by **lyre**
                     and **harp**, by **tambourine** and **flute**, and by
                     wine;
                     But they do not pay attention to the deeds
                     of the LORD,
                     Nor do they consider the work of His hands.

GOD'S SALVATION

12:1–6   2   "Behold, God is my salvation,
                     I will trust and not be afraid;
                     For the LORD GOD is my strength and **song**,
                     And He has become my salvation."
               5   Praise the LORD in **song**, for He has done

excellent things;
Let this be known throughout the earth.

TAUNT TO BABYLON

14:3–21   11   'Your pomp *and* the **music** of your **harps**
Have been brought down to Sheol;
Maggots are spread out *as your bed* beneath you,
And worms are your covering.'

MOAB

16:6–12   11   Therefore my heart **intones** like a **harp** for Moab,
And my inward feelings for Kir-hareseth.

CUSH

18:1–7   3   All you inhabitants of the world and dwellers on earth,
As soon as a standard is raised on the mountains, you will see *it,*
And as soon as the **trumpet** is **blown**, you will hear *it.*

TYRE

23:15–18   15 Now it will come about in that day that Tyre will be forgotten for seventy years like the days of one king. At the end of seventy years it will happen to Tyre as *in* the **song** of the harlot:

16   Take *your* **harp**, walk about the city, O forgotten harlot;
Pluck the **strings skillfully**, **sing** many **songs**,
That you may be remembered.

THE LORD'S JUDGMENT

24:7–23   8   The gaiety of **tambourines** ceases,
The noise of revelers stops,
The gaiety of the **harp** ceases.

9   They do not drink wine with **song**;
Strong drink is better to those who drink it.

16   From the ends of the earth we hear **songs**,

"Glory to the Righteous One,"
"But I say, "Woe to me! Woe to me! Alas
for me!
The treacherous deal treacherously,
And the treacherous deal very treacherously."

SONG IN JUDAH

26:1–6   1 In that day this **song** will be **sung** in the land of Judah:
              "We have a strong city;
              He sets up walls and ramparts for security.

SONG OF VICTORY

27:1–6   2 In that day,
              "A vineyard of wine, **sing** of it!

SONG OF VICTORY

27:12, 13   13 It will come about also in that day that a great **trum-
              pet** will be **blown**; and those who were perishing in the
              land of Assyria and who were scattered in the land of
              Egypt will come and worship the LORD in the holy moun-
              tain at Jerusalem.

THE LORD'S ANGER AGAINST THE NATIONS

30:27–33   29 You will have **songs** as in the night when
              you keep the festival;
              And gladness of heart as when one marches
              to *the sound of* the **flute**,
              To go to the mountain of the LORD, to the
              Rock of Israel.

              32 And every blow of the rod of punishment,
              Which the LORD will lay on him,
              Will be with *the music of* **tambourines** and
              lyres;
              And in battles, brandishing weapons, He will
              fight them.

PRAYER AND THANKSGIVING

38:10–20   20 "The LORD will surely save me;
              So we will **play** my **songs** on **stringed instruments**
              All *the* days of our life at the house of the LORD."

EXHORTATION TO PRAISE

42:10–13   10   **Sing** to the LORD a new **song**,
Sing His praise from the end of the earth!
You who go down to the sea, and all that is in it.
You islands and those who dwell on them.

               11   Let the wilderness and its cities lift up *their voices,*
The settlements where Kedar inhabits.
Let the inhabitants of Sela **sing** aloud,
Let them shout for joy from the tops of the mountains.

COMFORT BY THE LORD

51:1–3   3   Indeed, the LORD will comfort Zion;
He will comfort all her waste places.
And her wilderness He will make like Eden,
And her desert like the garden of the LORD;
Joy and gladness will be found in her,
Thanksgiving and **sound** of a **melody**.

A CALL TO RIGHTEOUSNESS

58:1   1   "Cry loudly, do not hold back;
Raise your voice like a **trumpet**,
And declare to My people their transgression,
And to the house of Jacob their sins.

JEREMIAH

Note: Much of Jeremiah is poetry, and as such might have been sung.

CALL TO REPENTANCE

4:5–8   5 Declare in Judah and proclaim in Jerusalem, and say,
"**Blow** the **trumpet** in the land;
Cry aloud and say,
'Assemble yourselves, and let us go
Into the fortified cities.'

SOUL ANGUISH

4:19–22

19 My soul, my soul! I am in anguish! Oh, my
heart!
My heart is pounding in me;
I cannot be silent,
Because you have heard, O my soul,
The **sound** of the **trumpet**,
The alarm of war.

21 How long must I see the standard,
And hear the **sound** of the **trumpet**?

WARNING OF GOD'S JUDGMENT

6:1–8

1 "Flee for safety, O sons of Benjamin,
From the midst of Jerusalem!
Now **blow** a **trumpet** in Tekoa,
And raise a signal over Beth-haccerem;
For evil looks down from the north,
And a great destruction.

WARNING OF GOD'S JUDGMENT

6:16–21

17 "And I set watchmen over you, *saying*,
'Listen to the **sound** of the **trumpet**!'
But they said, 'We will not listen.'

FALSE PROPHECY

20:7–13

13 **Sing** to the LORD, praise the LORD!
For He has delivered the soul of the needy
one
From the hand of evildoers.

DELIVERANCE BY THE LORD

31:1–9

4 "Again I will build you, and you shall be
rebuilt, O virgin of Israel!
Again you shall take up your **tambourines**,
And go forth to the **dances** of the merry-
makers.

7 For thus says the LORD,
"**Sing** aloud with gladness for Jacob,

(53

And shout among the chiefs of the nations;
Proclaim, give praise, and say,
'O *Lord*, save Thy people,
The remnant of Israel.'

PROPHECY TO THE NATIONS

31:10–14   13   "Then the virgin shall rejoice in the **dance**,
And the young men and the old, together,
For I will turn their mourning into joy,
And will comfort them, and give them joy
    for their sorrow.

PROMISES TO ISRAEL

42:7–17   14 saying, "No, but we will go to the land of Egypt,
where we shall not see war or hear the **sound** of a **trumpet**
or hunger for bread, and we will stay there";

SORROW FOR MOAB

48:36–44   36 "Therefore My heart **wails** for Moab like **flutes**; My
heart also **wails** like **flutes** for the men of Kir-heres.
Therefore they have lost the abundance it produced.

SUMMONS TO THE NATIONS

51:27–32   27   Lift up a signal in the land,
Blow a **trumpet** among the nations!
Consecrate the nations against her,
Summon against her the kingdoms of Ararat,
    Minni and Ashkenaz;
Appoint a marshal against her,
Bring up the horses like bristly locusts.

LAMENTATIONS

MOCKERY BY THE PEOPLE

3:1–18   14   I have become a laughingstock to all my people,
Their *mocking* **song** all the day.

MOCKERY BY THE PEOPLE

3:59–63   63   Look on their sitting and their rising

I am their mocking **song**.

RESULTS OF JUDGMENT

5:1–18

14 Elders are gone from the gate,
Young men from their **music**.
15 The joy of our hearts has ceased;
Our **dancing** has been turned into mourning.

EZEKIEL

PROPHECY

7:14–22

14 'They have **blown** the **trumpet** and made everything ready, but no one is going to the battle; for My wrath is against all their multitude.

PROPHECY ABOUT TYRE

26:7–14

13 "So I will silence the **sound** of your **songs**, and the **sound** of your **harps** will be heard no more.

THE WATCHMAN'S RESPONSIBILITY

33:1–6

3 and he sees the sword coming upon the land, and he **blows** on the **trumpet** and warns the people,
4 then he who hears the **sound** of the **trumpet** and does not take warning, and a sword comes and takes him away, his blood will be on his *own* head.
5 'He heard the **sound** of the **trumpet**, but did not take warning; his blood will be on himself. But had he taken warning, he would have delivered his life.
6 'But if the watchman sees the sword coming and does not **blow** the **trumpet**, and the people are not warned, and a sword comes and takes a person from them, he is taken away in his iniquity; but his blood I will require from the watchman's hand.'

HYPOCRISY

33:30–32

32 "And behold, you are to them like a sensual **song** by one who has a beautiful voice and **plays** well on an **instrument**; for they hear your words, but they do not practice them.

TEMPLE DESCRIPTIONS

40:44–47

44 And from the outside to the inner gate were chambers for the **singers** in the inner court, *one of* which was at the side of the north gate, with its front toward the south, and one at the side of the east gate facing toward the north.

DANIEL

NEBUCHADNEZZAR'S GOLD IMAGE

3:1–18

5 that at the moment you hear the **sound** of the **horn, flute, lyre, trigon, psaltery, bagpipe**, and all kinds of **music**, you are to fall down and worship the golden image that Nebuchadnezzar the king has set up.

7 Therefore at that time, when all the peoples heard the **sound** of the **horn, flute, lyre, trigon, psaltery, bagpipe**, and all kinds of **music**, all the peoples, nations and *men of every* language fell down *and* worshiped the golden image that Nebuchadnezzar the king had set up.

10 "You yourself, O king, have made a decree that every man who hears the **sound** of the **horn, flute, lyre, trigon, psaltery**, and **bagpipe**, and all kinds of **music**, is to fall down and worship the golden image.

15 "Now if you are ready, at the moment you hear the **sound** of the **horn, flute, lyre, trigon, psaltery**, and **bagpipe**, and all kinds of **music**, to fall down and worship the image that I have made, *very well*. But if you will not worship, you will immediately be cast into the midst of a furnace of blazing fire; and what god is there who can deliver you out of my hands?"

HOSEA

ISRAEL'S RESTORATION

2:14–20

15 "Then I will give her her vineyards from there,
And the valley of Achor as a door of hope.
And she will **sing** there as in the days of her youth,

As in the day when she came up from the land of
  Egypt.

JUDGMENT AGAINST ISRAEL

5:8–15   **8**   **Blow** the **horn** in Gibeah,
                         The **trumpet** in Ramah.
                         Sound an alarm at Beth-aven:
                         "Behind you, Benjamin!"

ISRAEL'S TRANSGRESSION

8:1–7   1   *Put* the **trumpet** to your lips!
                     Like an eagle *the enemy comes* against the house of
                       the LORD,
                     Because they have transgressed My covenant,
                     And rebelled against My law.

JOEL

PROPHECY

2:1–17   1   **Blow** a **trumpet** in Zion,
                     And **sound** an alarm on My holy mountain!
                     Let all the inhabitants of the land tremble,
                     For the day of the LORD is coming;
                     Surely it is near,

               15   **Blow** a **trumpet** in Zion,
                     Consecrate a fast, proclaim a solemn assembly,

AMOS

JUDGMENT ON MOAB

2:1–3   2   "So I will send fire upon Moab,
                     And it will consume the citadels of Kerioth;
                     And Moab will die amid tumult,
                     With war cries and the **sound** of a **trumpet**.

WITNESS AGAINST ISRAEL

3:2–8   6   If a **trumpet** is **blown** in a city will not the people

(57

tremble?
If a calamity occurs in a city has not the LORD
done it?

OFFERINGS REJECTED BY GOD

5:21–24   23   "Take away from Me the **noise** of your **songs**;
I will not even listen to the **sound** of your **harps**.

LIFESTYLE REJECTED BY GOD

6:4–7   5   Who **improvise** to the **sound** of the **harp,**
And like **David** have **composed songs** for them-
selves,

JUDGMENT ON ISRAEL

8:1–10   3 "The **songs** of the palace will turn to wailing in that
day," declares the Lord GOD. "Many *will be* the corpses; in
every place they will cast them forth in silence."

10   "Then I shall turn your festivals into mourning
And all your **songs** into lamentation;
And I will bring sackcloth on everyone's loins
And baldness on every head.
And I will make it like *a time of* mourning for an
only son,
And the end of it will be like a bitter day.

OBADIAH

JONAH

MICAH

NAHUM

HABAKKUK

Note : All of Habakkuk is the text of a song.

JUDGMENT FOR GREED

2:6–8   **6**   "Will not all of these take up a **taunt-song**
against him,
Even mockery *and* insinuations against him,
And say, 'Woe to him who increases what is
not his—
For how long—
And makes himself rich with loans?'

SHIGIONOTH

3:1   1 A prayer of Habakkuk the prophet, according to
Shigionoth.

SELAH

3:3, 9, 13

RESOLUTION TO REJOICE

3:16–19   19   The Lord GOD is my strength,
And He has made my feet like hinds' *feet,*
And makes me walk on my high places.

For the **choir director**, on my **stringed instruments.**

ZEPHANIAH

THE DAY OF THE LORD

1:14–18   16   A day of **trumpet** and battle cry,
Against the fortified cities
And the high corner towers.

JUDGMENT AGAINST THE NATIONS

2:12–15   14   And flocks will lie down in her midst
All beasts which range in herds;

> Both the pelican and the hedgehog
> Will lodge in the tops of her pillars;
> Birds will **sing** in the window,
> Desolation *will be* on the threshold;
> For He has laid bare the cedar work.

HAGGAI

ZECHARIAH

THE LORD'S PRESENCE PROMISED

2:6–13   10 "**Sing** for joy and be glad, O daughter of Zion; for behold I am coming and I will dwell in your midst," declares the LORD.

THE LORD'S HELP IN CONQUEST

9:11–17   14   Then the LORD will appear over them,
> And His arrow will go forth like lightning;
> And the Lord GOD will **blow** the **trumpet**,
> And will march in the storm winds of the south.

MALACHI

New Testament

Matthew

GIVING OF ALMS

6:1–4   2 "When therefore you give alms, do not **sound** a **trumpet** before you, as the hypocrites do in the synagogues and in the streets, that they may be honored by men. Truly I say to you, they have their reward in full.

GIRL RAISED FROM THE DEAD

9:18–26   23 And when Jesus came into the official's house, and saw the **flute-players**, and the crowd in noisy disorder,

JESUS SPEAKING OF JOHN THE BAPTIST

11:7–19   17 and say, 'We **played** the **flute** for you, and you did not **dance**; we **sang** a **dirge**, and you did not mourn.'

HEROD'S DAUGHTER

14:1–12   6 But when Herod's birthday came, the daughter of Herodias **danced** before *them* and pleased Herod.

END-TIME PROPHECY

24:29–31   31 "And He will send forth His angels with A GREAT TRUMPET and THEY WILL GATHER TOGETHER His elect from the four winds, from one end of the sky to the other.

LAST SUPPER

26:26–30   30 And after **singing** a **hymn**, they went out to the Mount of Olives.

MARK

HERODIAS'S DAUGHTER

6:14–29   22 and when the daughter of Herodias herself came in and **danced**, she pleased Herod and his dinner guests; and the king said to the girl, "Ask me for whatever you want and I will give it to you."

LAST SUPPER

14:22–26   26 And after **singing** a **hymn**, they went out to the Mount of Olives.

LUKE

JESUS SPEAKING OF JOHN THE BAPTIST

7:24–35   32 "They are like children who sit in the market place and call to one another; and they say, 'We **played** the **flute** for you, and you did not **dance**; we **sang** a **dirge**, and you did not weep.'

THE PRODIGAL SON

15:11–32   25 "Now his older son was in the field, and when he came and approached the house, he heard **music** and **dancing**.

JESUS, DAVID'S SON

20:41–44   42 "For **David** himself says in the book of **Psalms**,
                    'THE LORD SAID TO MY LORD,
                    "SIT AT MY RIGHT HAND,

JESUS EXPOUNDS THE SCRIPTURES

24:44–49   44 Now He said to them, "These are My words which I spoke to you while I was still with you, that all things which are written about Me in the Law of Moses and the Prophets and the **Psalms** must be fulfilled."

JOHN

ACTS

PETER SPEAKS

1:15–26

20 "For it is written in the book of **Psalms**,
    'LET HIS HOMESTEAD BE MADE DESOLATE,
    AND LET NO MAN DWELL IN IT';
and,
    'HIS OFFICE LET ANOTHER MAN TAKE.'

PAUL PREACHES

13:16–41

33 that God has fulfilled this *promise* to our children in
that He raised up Jesus, as it is also written in the second
Psalm, 'THOU ART MY SON; TODAY I HAVE BEGOTTEN
THEE.'

35 "Therefore He also says in another **Psalm**, 'THOU
WILT NOT ALLOW THY HOLY ONE TO UNDERGO DECAY.'

PAUL AND SILAS IN PRISON

16:19–40

25 But about midnight Paul and Silas were praying and
singing hymns of praise to God, and the prisoners were
listening to them;

ROMANS

OLD TESTAMENT QUOTES

15:7–13

9 and for the Gentiles to glorify God for His
mercy; as it is written,
    "THEREFORE I WILL GIVE PRAISE TO THEE
    AMONG THE GENTILES,
    AND I WILL **SING** TO THY NAME."

1 CORINTHIANS

LOVE

13:1–3   1 If I speak with the tongues of men and of angels, but do not have love, I have become a **noisy gong** or a **clanging cymbal**.

SPIRITUAL GIFTS

14:1–33   7 Yet *even* lifeless things, either **flute** or **harp**, in producing a **sound**, if they do not produce a **distinction** in the **tones**, how will it be known what is **played** on the **flute** or on the **harp**?

8 For if the **bugle** produces an **indistinct sound**, who will prepare himself for battle?

15 What is *the outcome* then? I shall pray with the spirit and I shall pray with the mind also; I shall **sing** with the spirit and I shall **sing** with the mind also.

26 What is *the outcome* then, brethren? When you assemble, each one has a **psalm**, has a teaching, has a revelation, has a tongue, has an interpretation. Let all things be done for edification.

JESUS' SECOND COMING

15:50–58   52 in a moment, in the twinkling of an eye, at the last **trumpet**; for the **trumpet** will **sound**, and the dead will be raised imperishable, and we shall be changed.

2 CORINTHIANS

GALATIANS

EPHESIANS

FILLING OF THE SPIRIT

5:15–21   19 speaking to one another in **psalms** and **hymns** and spiritual **songs, singing** and making **melody** with your heart to the Lord;

PHILIPPIANS

COLOSSIANS

HOLY LIVING

3:12–17   16 Let the word of Christ richly dwell within you, with all wisdom teaching and admonishing one another with **psalms** *and* **hymns** *and* spiritual **songs, singing** with **thankfulness** in your hearts to God.

1 THESSALONIANS

JESUS' SECOND COMING

4:13–18   16 For the Lord Himself will descend from heaven with a shout, with the voice of *the* archangel, and with the **trumpet** of God; and the dead in Christ shall rise first.

2 THESSALONIANS

1 TIMOTHY

2 TIMOTHY

TITUS

PHILEMON

HEBREWS

JESUS FELLOWSHIPS WITH THE BRETHREN

2:5–18   12 saying,

"I WILL PROCLAIM THY NAME TO MY BRETHREN,
IN THE MIDST OF THE CONGREGATION I WILL
SING THY PRAISE."

GIVING OF THE COMMANDMENTS

12:18–29   19 and to the **blast** of a **trumpet** and the **sound** of words which *sound was such that* those who heard begged that no further word should be spoken to them.

JAMES

HEALING FOR THE SICK

5:13–18   13 Is anyone among you suffering? Let him pray. Is anyone cheerful? Let him **sing** praises.

1 PETER

2 PETER

1 JOHN

2 JOHN

3 JOHN

JUDE

REVELATION

THE VOICE OF THE LORD

1:9–20   10 I was in the Spirit on the Lord's day, and I heard behind me a loud voice like *the sound* of a **trumpet**,

THE THRONE IN HEAVEN

4:1–11   1 After these things I looked, and behold, a door *standing* open in heaven, and the first voice which I had heard, like *the sound* of a **trumpet** speaking with me, said, "Come up here, and I will show you what must take place after these things."

THE LAMB AND THE SCROLL

5:1–14   8 And when He had taken the book, the four living creatures and the twenty-four elders fell down before the Lamb, having each one a **harp**, and golden bowls full of incense, which are the prayers of the saints.

9 And they **sang* a new **song**, saying,

"Worthy art Thou to take the book, and to break its seals; for Thou wast slain, and didst purchase for God with Thy blood *men* from every tribe and tongue and people and nation.

THE SEVEN TRUMPETS

8:2–13   2 And I saw the seven angels who stand before God; and seven **trumpets** were given to them.

6 And the seven angels who had the seven **trumpets** prepared themselves to **sound** them.

7 And the first **sounded**, and there came hail and fire, mixed with blood, and they were thrown to the earth; and a third of the earth was burned up, and a third of the trees were burned up, and all the green grass was burned up.

8 And the second angel **sounded**, and *something* like a great mountain burning with fire was thrown into the sea; and a third of the sea became blood;

10 And the third angel **sounded**, and a great star fell

from heaven, burning like a torch, and it fell on a third of the rivers and on the springs of waters;

12 And the fourth angel **sounded**, and a third of the sun and a third of the moon and a third of the stars were smitten, so that a third of them might be darkened and the day might not shine for a third of it, and the night in the same way.

THE SEVEN TRUMPETS

9:1–21

1 And the fifth angel **sounded**, and I saw a star from heaven which had fallen to the earth; and the key of the bottomless pit was given to him.

13 And the sixth angel **sounded**, and I heard a voice from the four horns of the golden altar which is before God,

14 one saying to the sixth angel who had the **trumpet**, "Release the four angels who are bound at the great river Euphrates."

THE SEVEN TRUMPETS

10:1–11

7 but in the days of the voice of the seventh angel, when he is about to **sound**, then the mystery of God is finished, as He preached to His servants the prophets.

THE SEVEN TRUMPETS

11:1–15

15 And the seventh angel **sounded**; and there arose loud voices in heaven, saying,

"The kingdom of the world has become *the kingdom* of our Lord, and of His Christ; and He will reign forever and ever."

THE 144,000

14:1–5

2 And I heard a voice from heaven, like the **sound** of many waters and like the **sound** of loud thunder, and the voice which I heard *was* like *the sound* of **harpists playing** on their **harps.**

3 And they *sang a new **song** before the throne and before the four living creatures and the elders; and no one could learn the **song** except the one hundred and forty-

four thousand who had been purchased from the earth.

SEVEN ANGELS AND SEVEN PLAGUES

15:1–4

2 And I saw, as it were, a sea of glass mixed with fire, and those who had come off victorious from the beast and from his image and from the number of his name, standing on the sea of glass, holding **harps** of God.

3 And they ***sang** the **song** of **Moses** the bond-servant of God and the **song** of the Lamb, saying,

"Great and marvelous are Thy works,
O Lord God, the Almighty;
Righteous and true are Thy ways,
Thou King of the nations.

BABYLON DEFEATED

18:21–24

22 "And the **sound** of **harpists** and **musicians** and **flute-players** and **trumpeters** will not be heard in you any longer; and no craftsman of any craft will be found in you any longer; and the sound of a mill will not be heard in you any longer;

Part Two
Topical Concordance

EXPLANATION OF ENTRIES

Entries where the actual word appears in the references are set in bold face. When an idea or topic and not the actual word is used in a reference, the print will be in normal face (i.e., the word **accompaniment** appears in the text of Psalm 5:0; the idea or topic of accompaniment is suggested in Exodus 15:1, 1 Samuel 10:5, etc.).

Accompanied
  2 Chronicles 5:13
  2 Chronicles 29:27
  Isaiah 5:12
see also **Accompaniment**,
Accompaniment

Accompaniment
  Psalm 5:0
see also **Accompanied**, Accompaniment

Accompaniment
  Exodus 15:1
  1 Samuel 10:5
  Job 21:12
  Psalm 12:0
  Psalm 33:2, 3
  Psalm 71:22
  Psalm 92:3
  Psalm 98:5, 6
  Psalm 147:7
  Psalm 149:3
  Isaiah 23:16
  Ezekiel 33:32
  Revelation 5:8, 9
see also **Accompanied, Accompaniment**

Aijeleth Hashshahar
  (*the hind of the morning*)
  Psalm 22:0

Alamoth
  (possibly *for soprano voices*)
  1 Chronicles 15:20
  Psalm 46:0

Al-Tashhethai
  (*do not destroy*)
  Psalm 57:0
  Psalm 58:0
  Psalm 59:0
  Psalm 75:0

Amasai
  1 Chronicles 15:24

Angels
  Revelation 8:2–11:19

Asaph
  1 Chronicles 6:39
  1 Chronicles 15:19
  1 Chronicles 16:5

1 Chronicles 25:1, 2, 6
2 Chronicles 5:12
2 Chronicles 29:30
2 Chronicles 35:15
Ezra 2:41
Ezra 3:10
Nehemiah 7:44
Nehemiah 11:22
Psalm 50:0
Psalm 73:0
Psalm 74:0
Psalm 75:0
Psalm 76:0
Psalm 77:0
Psalm 78:0
Psalm 79:0
Psalm 80:0
Psalm 81:0
Psalm 82:0
Psalm 83:0

Ascents
Psalm 120:0
Psalm 121:0
Psalm 122:0
Psalm 123:0
Psalm 124:0
Psalm 125:0
Psalm 126:0
Psalm 127:0
Psalm 128:0
Psalm 129:0
Psalm 130:0
Psalm 131:0
Psalm 132:0
Psalm 133:0
Psalm 134:0

Asharelah
1 Chronicles 25:2

Assembly
Exodus 15:1–21
Exodus 19:10–17

Exodus 20:18–21
Leviticus 23:36
Numbers 1–10
2 Chronicles 5:11–14
2 Chronicles 15:14
2 Chronicles 29:20–36
2 Chronicles 30:13–23
Psalm 68:24–27
Psalm 150:1–6
Jeremiah 4:5–8
Joel 1:2

Azarel
Nehemiah 12:36

Azaziah
1 Chronicles 15:21

Aziel
1 Chronicles 15:20

Bagpipe
Daniel 3:5
Daniel 3:7
Daniel 3:10
Daniel 3:15

Barak
Judges 4:6–5:31

Beating
Psalm 68:25
see also **Strike**

Benaiah
1 Chronicles 15:20, 24
1 Chronicles 16:5, 6

Blast
Exodus 19:13
Joshua 6:5
Hebrews 12:19

Blew

Joshua 6:8, 9, 16, 20
Judges 3:27
Judges 7:19, 20, 22
1 Samuel 13:3
2 Samuel 2:28
2 Samuel 18:16
2 Samuel 20:1, 22
1 Kings 1:39
2 Kings 9:13
2 Kings 11:14
1 Chronicles 15:24
1 Chronicles 16:6
2 Chronicles 7:6
2 Chronicles 13:14
2 Chronicles 23:13
see also **Blow, Blowing, Blown, Blows**

Blow

Numbers 10:5, 6, 7, 8, 10
Joshua 6:4, 9, 13
Judges 7:18
1 Kings 1:34
Psalm 81:3
Jeremiah 4:5
Jeremiah 6:1
Jeremiah 51:27
Ezekiel 33:6
Hosea 5:8
Joel 2:1
see also **Blew, Blowing, Blown, Blows**

Blowing

Leviticus 23:24
Numbers 29:1
Judges 7:20
2 Chronicles 5:12
see also **Blew, Blow, Blown, Blows**

Blown

Numbers 10:3, 4
Isaiah 18:3
Isaiah 27:13
Amos 3:6

see also **Blew, Blow, Blowing, Blows**

Blows

Ezekiel 33:3
see also **Blew, Blow, Blowing, Blown**

Bugle

1 Corinthians 14:8

Bukkaiah

1 Chronicles 25:4

Castanets

2 Samuel 6:5

Celebration

Genesis 31:27
Exodus 15:1–21
Judges 5:1–31
Judges 11:34
2 Samuel 6:5–23
1 Kings 1:32–48
2 Kings 11:12–14
1 Chronicles 13:8
1 Chronicles 15:27–28
1 Chronicles 16:1–43
2 Chronicles 30:21
Nehemiah 12:27–47
Psalm 81:1–5
Isaiah 30:29
Luke 15:22–25

Chanted

2 Samuel 1:17
2 Samuel 3:33
2 Chronicles 35:25
see also **Dirge. Lament**

Chenaniah

1 Chronicles 15:22

Choir Director

Psalm 4:0
Psalm 5:0

Psalm 6:0
Psalm 8:0
Psalm 9:0
Psalm 11:0
Psalm 12:0
Psalm 13:0
Psalm 14:0
Psalm 18:0
Psalm 19:0
Psalm 20:0
Psalm 21:0
Psalm 22:0
Psalm 31:0
Psalm 36:0
Psalm 39:0
Psalm 40:0
Psalm 41:0
Psalm 42:0
Psalm 44:0
Psalm 45:0
Psalm 46:0
Psalm 47:0
Psalm 49:0
Psalm 51:0
Psalm 52:0
Psalm 53:0
Psalm 54:0
Psalm 55:0
Psalm 56:0
Psalm 57:0
Psalm 58:0
Psalm 59:0
Psalm 60:0
Psalm 61:0
Psalm 62:0
Psalm 64:0
Psalm 65:0
Psalm 66:0
Psalm 67:0
Psalm 68:0
Psalm 69:0
Psalm 70:0
Psalm 75:0
Psalm 76:0

Psalm 77:0
Psalm 80:0
Psalm 81:0
Psalm 84:0
Psalm 85:0
Psalm 88:0
Psalm 109:0
Psalm 139:0
Psalm 140:0
Habakkuk 3:19

Choirs
   Nehemiah 12:31–40

Clanging
   1 Corinthians 13:1

Composed
   Amos 6:5
see also Composition, **Psalmist**

Composition
   Exodus 15:1
   Deuteronomy 31:19–22
   Deuteronomy 32:1–47
   1 Samuel 18:6, 7
   2 Samuel 1:17, 18
   Psalm 33:3
   Psalm 40:3
   Psalm 98:1
   Psalm 144:9
   Song of Solomon 1:1
   Isaiah 42:10–13
   Amos 6:5
   Revelation 5:9
   Revelation 14:3
see also **Composed, Psalmist**

Cymbal
   1 Corinthians 13:1
see also **Cymbals**

Cymbals
   2 Samuel 6:5

1 Chronicles 13:8
1 Chronicles 15:16, 19, 28
1 Chronicles 16:5, 42
1 Chronicles 25:1
2 Chronicles 29:25
Ezra 3:10
Nehemiah 12:27
Psalm 150:5
see also **Cymbal**

Dance
Ecclesiastes 3:4
Jeremiah 31:13
Matthew 11:17
Luke 7:32
see also **Danced, Dances, Dancing**

Danced
Judges 21:23
1 Samuel 21:11
Matthew 14:6
Mark 6:22
see also **Dance, Dances, Dancing**

Dances
Judges 21:21
1 Samuel 29:5
Jeremiah 31:4
see also **Dance, Danced, Dancing**

Dancing
Exodus 15:20
Exodus 32:19
Judges 11:34
1 Samuel 18:6
1 Samuel 30:16
2 Samuel 6:14, 16
Psalm 30:11
Psalm 149:3
Psalm 150:4
Lamentations 5:15
Luke 15:25
see also **Dance, Danced, Dances**

David
1 Samuel 18:10
1 Samuel 19:9
1 Chronicles 6:31
1 Chronicles 13:8
1 Chronicles 15:16, 27
1 Chronicles 25:1
2 Chronicles 7:6
2 Chronicles 29:25, 26, 27, 30
2 Chronicles 36:15
Ezra 3:10
Nehemiah 12:36, 45, 46
Psalm 3:0
Psalm 4:0
Psalm 5:0
Psalm 6:0
Psalm 7:0
Psalm 8:0
Psalm 9:0
Psalm 11:0
Psalm 12:0
Psalm 13:0
Psalm 14:0
Psalm 15:0
Psalm 16:0
Psalm 17:0
Psalm 18:0
Psalm 19:0
Psalm 20:0
Psalm 21:0
Psalm 22:0
Psalm 23:0
Psalm 24:0
Psalm 25:0
Psalm 26:0
Psalm 27:0
Psalm 28:0
Psalm 29:0
Psalm 30:0
Psalm 31:0
Psalm 32:0
Psalm 34:0
Psalm 35:0
Psalm 36:0

Psalm 37:0
Psalm 38:0
Psalm 39:0
Psalm 40:0
Psalm 41:0
Psalm 51:0
Psalm 52:0
Psalm 53:0
Psalm 54:0
Psalm 55:0
Psalm 56:0
Psalm 57:0
Psalm 58:0
Psalm 59:0
Psalm 60:0
Psalm 61:0
Psalm 62:0
Psalm 63:0
Psalm 64:0
Psalm 65:0
Psalm 68:0
Psalm 69:0
Psalm 70:0
Psalm 86:0
Psalm 101:0
Psalm 103:0
Psalm 108:0
Psalm 109:0
Psalm 110:0
Psalm 122:0
Psalm 124:0
Psalm 131:0
Psalm 133:0
Psalm 138:0
Psalm 139:0
Psalm 140:0
Psalm 141:0
Psalm 142:0
Psalm 143:0
Psalm 144:0
Psalm 145:0

David
  1 Samuel 16:14–23

2 Samuel 1:17–27
2 Samuel 22:1–51

Deborah
  Judges 5:1–31

Dirge
  Matthew 11:17
  Luke 7:32
  see also **Chanted, Lament**

Distinction
  1 Corinthians 14:7

Dress
  1 Chronicles 15:27
  2 Chronicles 5:12
  2 Chronicles 20:21
  Ezra 3:10

Dynamics
  Exodus 19:16, 19
  Joshua 6:1–20
  1 Kings 1:39–41
  1 Chronicles 15:16, 28
  2 Chronicles 30:21
  Psalm 150:5
  Ecclesiastes 12:4
  Isaiah 42:11
  Isaiah 58:1
  Jeremiah 31:7
  see also Sound quality

Eduth
  Psalm 60:0
  Psalm 80:0

Ehud
  Judges 3:26–30

Eight-stringed
  Psalm 6:0
  Psalm 12:0
  see also **Ten-stringed, Ten strings**

Elam
Nehemiah 12:42

Eleazar
Nehemiah 12:42

Eliab
1 Chronicles 15:20
1 Chronicles 16:5

Eliakim
Nehemiah 12:41

Eliashib
Ezra 10:24

Eliathah
1 Chronicles 25:4

Eliezer
1 Chronicles 15:24

Elioenai
Nehemiah 12:41

Eliphelehu
1 Chronicles 15:21

El Shoshannim
Psalm 80:0

Emotions
Genesis 31:27
Exodus 19:16
Exodus 20:18
1 Samuel 18:6
2 Samuel 1:17–27
2 Samuel 3:31–39
1 Kings 1:39–41
1 Chronicles 16:33
2 Chronicles 23:18
2 Chronicles 29:30
2 Chronicles 30:21
2 Chronicles 35:25
Nehemiah 12:27–47

Job 21:12
Job 29:13
Job 38:7
Job 39:24, 25
Psalm 9:2
Psalm 27:6
Psalm 28:7
Psalm 40:3
Psalm 43:4
Psalm 51:14
Psalm 59:16, 17
Psalm 65:13
Psalm 67:4
Psalm 71:22–24
Psalm 77:6
Psalm 81:1–3
Psalm 87:7
Psalm 92:4
Psalm 95:1, 2
Psalm 98:4–6, 8
Psalm 100:1, 2, 4
Psalm 138:2–4
Psalm 149:5
Proverbs 25:20
Proverbs 29:6
Ecclesiastes 3:4
Isaiah 16:11
Isaiah 24:8, 9
Isaiah 30:29
Isaiah 42:10, 11
Isaiah 51:3
Jeremiah 4:19
Jeremiah 48:36
Lamentations 5:15
Ezekiel 7:14
Amos 8:3, 10
Matthew 11:17
Luke 7:32
Ephesians 5:19
James 5:13

Ethan
1 Kings 4:31
1 Chronicles 15:19

Ethan the Ezrahite
Psalm 89:0

Ezer
Nehemiah 12:42

Figures of speech
1 Chronicles 16:33
Job 29:13
Job 30:31
Job 38:7
Psalm 49:4
Psalm 57:8
Psalm 65:13
Psalm 98:8
Psalm 108:2
Proverbs 25:20
Isaiah 16:11
Isaiah 23:14
Isaiah 24:7, 8
Isaiah 30:29
Isaiah 42:11
Isaiah 58:1
Jeremiah 48:36
Ezekiel 33:32
Hosea 2:15
Luke 7:32
1 Corinthians 13:1
Revelation 1:10
Revelation 4:1
Revelation 14:2

Flute
1 Samuel 10:5
Job 21:12
Job 30:31
Psalm 5:0
Isaiah 5:12
Isaiah 30:29
Daniel 3:5, 7, 10, 15
Matthew 11:17
Luke 7:32
1 Corinthians 14:7
see also **Flute-players, Flutes**

Flute-players
Revelation 18:22
see also **Flute, Flutes**

Flutes
1 Kings 1:40
Psalm 87:7
Jeremiah 48:36
see also **Flute, Flute-players**

Gedaliah
1 Chronicles 25:3

Giddalti
1 Chronicles 25:4

Gilalai
Nehemiah 12:36

Gittith
Psalm 8:0
Psalm 81:0
Psalm 84:0

Gong
1 Corinthians 13:1

Hanani
1 Chronicles 25:4
Nehemiah 12:36

Hananiah
1 Chronicles 25:4
Nehemiah 12:41

Harp
1 Samuel 10:5
1 Samuel 16:16, 23
1 Samuel 18:10
1 Samuel 19:9
1 Chronicles 25:3
Job 21:12
Job 30:31
Psalm 33:2

Psalm 49:4
Psalm 57:8
Psalm 71:22
Psalm 81:2
Psalm 92:3
Psalm 108:2
Psalm 144:9
Psalm 150:3
Isaiah 5:12
Isaiah 16:11
Isaiah 23:16
Isaiah 24:8
Amos 6:5
1 Corinthians 14:7
Revelation 5:8
see also **Harpists, Harps**

Harpists
Revelation 14:2
Revelation 18:22
see also **Harp, Harps**

Harps
2 Samuel 6:5
1 Kings 10:12
1 Chronicles 13:8
1 Chronicles 15:16, 20, 28
1 Chronicles 16:5
1 Chronicles 25:1, 6
2 Chronicles 5:12
2 Chronicles 9:11
2 Chronicles 20:28
2 Chronicles 29:25
Nehemiah 12:27
Psalm 137:2
Isaiah 14:11
Ezekiel 26:13
Amos 5:23
Revelation 14:2
Revelation 15:2
see also **Harp, Harpists**

Hashabiah
1 Chronicles 25:3

Heman
1 Kings 4:31
1 Chronicles 6:33
1 Chronicles 15:19
1 Chronicles 16:42
1 Chronicles 25:1, 4–6
2 Chronicles 5:12
2 Chronicles 35:15

Heman the Ezrahite
Psalm 88:0

Higgaion Selah
Psalm 9:16

Horn
Leviticus 25:9
Judges 3:27
1 Chronicles 15:28
Psalm 98:6
Daniel 3:5, 7, 10, 15
Hosea 5:8
see also **Horns**

Horns
2 Chronicles 15:14
Psalm 75:10
see also **Horn**

Hothir
1 Chronicles 25:4

Hymn
Matthew 26:30
Mark 14:26
see also **Hymns, Melody, Psalm, Psalms, Song, Songs, Taunt-song**

Hymns
Nehemiah 12:27, 46
Acts 16:25
Ephesians 5:19
Colossians 3:16
see also **Hymn, Melody, Psalm, Psalms,**

Song, Songs, Taunt-song

Improvise
Amos 6:5
see also **Beating, Intones, Play, Played, Playing, Plays, Strike**

Indistinct
1 Corinthians 14:8

Instrument
Ezekiel 33:32
see also **Bagpipe, Bugle, Castanets, Cymbal, Cymbals, Flute, Flutes, Gong, Harp, Harps, Horn, Horns, Instruments, Lute, Lyre, Lyres, Pipe, Psaltery, Ram's horn, Ram's horns, Stringed instruments, Strings, Tambourine, Timbrel, Timbrels, Trigon, Trumpet, Trumpets**

Instrument construction
2 Samuel 6:5
1 Kings 10:12
1 Chronicles 23:5
2 Chronicles 9:11

Instruments
1 Samuel 18:6
2 Samuel 6:5
1 Chronicles 15:16
1 Chronicles 16:5, 42
1 Chronicles 23:5
2 Chronicles 5:13
2 Chronicles 7:6
2 Chronicles 23:13
2 Chronicles 29:26, 27
2 Chronicles 30:21
2 Chronicles 34:12
Nehemiah 12:36
Psalm 150:4
Isaiah 13:5
Isaiah 38:20
Habakkuk 3:19

see also **Bagpipe, Bugle, Castanets, Cymbal, Cymbals, Flute, Flutes, Gong, Harp, Harps, Horn, Horns, Instrument, Lute, Lyre, Lyres, Pipe, Psaltery, Ram's horn, Ram's horns, Stringed instruments, Strings, Tambourine, Timbrel, Timbrels, Trigon, Trumpet, Trumpets**

Intones
Isaiah 16:11
see also **Beating, Play, Played, Playing, Plays, Strike**

Jahath
2 Chronicles 34:12

Jahaziel
1 Chronicles 16:6

Jeduthun
1 Chronicles 16:42
1 Chronicles 25:6
2 Chronicles 5:12

Jeduthun
(Ethan the Ezrahite)
Psalm 39:0
Psalm 62:0
Psalm 77:0

Jehiah
1 Chronicles 15:24

Jehiel
1 Chronicles 15:20
1 Chronicles 16:5

Jehohanan
Nehemiah 12:42

Jeiel
1 Chronicles 15:21
1 Chronicles 16:5

Jeremiah
2 Chronicles 35:25

Jerimoth
1 Chronicles 25:4

Jeshaiah
1 Chronicles 25:3

Jezrahiah
Nehemiah 12:42

Joab
2 Samuel 2:28
2 Samuel 18:16
2 Samuel 20:22

Jonath Elem Rehokim
(probably *to the tune of "The Silent Dove in Far-off Lands"*)
Psalm 56:0

Joseph
1 Chronicles 25:2

Joshaphat
1 Chronicles 15:24

Joshbekashah
1 Chronicles 25:4

Jubal
Genesis 4:21

Judah
Nehemiah 12:36

Korah, sons of
Psalm 42:0
Psalm 44:0
Psalm 45:0
Psalm 46:0
Psalm 47:0
Psalm 48:0
Psalm 49:0

Psalm 84:0
Psalm 85:0
Psalm 87:0
Psalm 88:0

Lament
2 Samuel 1:17
2 Samuel 3:31, 33
2 Chronicles 35:25
see also **Chanted**, **Dirge**

Leadership
Exodus 15:1
Exodus 15:20, 21
1 Chronicles 6:31–48
1 Chronicles 9:33
1 Chronicles 15:16–29
1 Chronicles 16:1–43
1 Chronicles 25:1–31
2 Chronicles 23:18
2 Chronicles 34:12
Ezra 3:8–13
Nehemiah 11:22–24
Nehemiah 12:27–47
Habakkuk 3:19

Levites
1 Chronicles 9:33
2 Chronicles 30:21
2 Chronicles 34:12
2 Chronicles 35:15

Levites
1 Chronicles 6:31–48
1 Chronicles 13:1–6
1 Chronicles 15:16–29
1 Chronicles 16:1–43
1 Chronicles 25:1–31
2 Chronicles 5:11–14
2 Chronicles 6:4–7
2 Chronicles 23:16–21
Ezra 2:1–70
Ezra 3:8–13
Ezra 7:11–26

Nehemiah 12:27–47
Nehemiah 13:4–14

Loud-sounding
1 Chronicles 15:16, 28
1 Chronicles 16:5

Lute
Psalm 92:3

Lyre
Genesis 4:21
Genesis 31:27
1 Samuel 10:5
Psalm 33:2
Psalm 43:4
Psalm 57:8
Psalm 71:22
Psalm 81:2
Psalm 92:3
Psalm 98:5
Psalm 108:2
Psalm 147:7
Psalm 149:3
Psalm 150;3
Isaiah 5:12
Daniel 3:5, 7, 10, 15

Lyres
2 Samuel 6:5
1 Kings 10:12
1 Chronicles 13:8
1 Chronicles 15:16, 21, 28
1 Chronicles 16:5
1 Chronicles 26:1, 6
2 Chronicles 5:12
2 Chronicles 9:11
2 Chronicles 20:28
2 Chronicles 29:25
Nehemiah 12:27
Isaiah 30:32

Maai
Nehemiah 12:36

Maaseiah
1 Chronicles 15:20
Nehemiah 12:42

Mahalath
(*sickness, a sad tone*)
Psalm 53:0

Mahalath Leannoth
Psalm 88:0

Mahazioth
1 Chronicles 25:4

Malchijah
Nehemiah 12:42

Mallothi
1 Chronicles 25:4

Maskil
(possibly *contemplative* or *didactic* or *skillful psalm*)
Psalm 32:0
Psalm 42:0
Psalm 44:0
Psalm 45:0
Psalm 52:0
Psalm 53:0
Psalm 54:0
Psalm 55:0
Psalm 74:0
Psalm 78:0
Psalm 88:0
Psalm 89:0
Psalm 142:0

Mattaniah
1 Chronicles 25:4

Mattithiah
1 Chronicles 15:21
1 Chronicles 16:5
1 Chronicles 25:3

Melody
Psalm 98:5
Isaiah 51:3
Ephesians 5:19
see also **Hymn, Hymns, Psalm, Psalms, Song, Songs, Taunt-song**

Merari
2 Chronicles 34:12

Meshullam
2 Chronicles 34:12

Micaiah
Nehemiah 12:41

Mikhtam
(possibly *epigrammatic poem* or *atonement psalm*)
Psalm 16:0
Psalm 56:0
Psalm 57:0
Psalm 58:0
Psalm 59:0
Psalm 60:0

Mikneiah
1 Chronicles 15:21

Milalai
Nehemiah 12:36

Miniamin
Nehemiah 12:41

Minstrel
2 Kings 3:15

Moses
Psalm 90:0
Revelation 15:3

Moses
Exodus 15:1–21

Deuteronomy 31:19–22
Deuteronomy 32:1–43

Music
1 Chronicles 15:16
2 Chronicles 5:13
2 Chronicles 7:6
Psalm 92:3
Isaiah 30:32
Lamentations 5:14
Daniel 3:5, 7, 10, 15
Luke 15:25

Musical instruments
1 Samuel 18:6
1 Chronicles 16:5
2 Chronicles 23:13
2 Chronicles 29:26
2 Chronicles 34:12
Nehemiah 12:36

Musician
1 Samuel 16:18
see also **Musicians,** Musicians

Musicians
Psalm 68:25
Revelation 18:22
see also **Musician,** Musicians

Musicians
see **Amasai,** Angels, **Asaph, Asharelah, Azarel, Azaziah, Aziel,** Barak, **Benaiah, Bukkiah, Chenaniah, David,** Deborah, Ehud, **Elam, Eleazar, Eliab, Eliakim, Eliashib, Eliathah, Eliezer, Elioenaei, Eliphelehu, Ethan, Ezer, Gedeliah, Giddalti, Gilalai, Hanani, Hananiah, Hashabiah, Heman, Hothir, Jahath, Jahaziel, Jeduthun, Jehiah, Jehiel, Jehohanan, Jeiel, Jeremiah, Jerimoth, Jeshaiah, Jezrahiah, Joab, Joseph, Joshaphat, Joshbekashah, Jubal, Judah, Maai, Maaseiah, Mahazioth,**

Malchijah, Mallothi, Mattaniah,
Mattithiah, Merari, Meshullam,
Micaiah, Mikneiah, Milalai, Miniamin,
Moses, Nethanel, Nethaniah, Obadiah,
Obed-Edom, Romamti-Ezer, Saul,
Sheba, Shebaniah, Shebuel, Shemaiah,
Shemiramoth, Shimei, Solomon, Unni,
Uzzi, Uzziel, Zaccur, Zechariah, Zeri

Muth-labben
(*death to the son*)
Psalm 9:0

Nethanel
Nehemiah 12:36
1 Chronicles 15:24

Nethaniah
1 Chronicles 25:2

Noise
Amos 5:23

Noisy
1 Corinthians 13:1

Obadiah
2 Chronicles 34:12

Obed-Edom
1 Chronicles 15:21, 24
1 Chronicles 16:5

Orchestra
1 Samuel 10:5
1 Chronicles 13:8
Nehemiah 12:27–47
Daniel 3:1–18

Pipe
Genesis 4:21
Psalm 150:4

Piping
Judges 5:16

Play
Genesis 4:21
1 Samuel 16:16, 17, 23
Psalm 33:3
Psalm 87:7
Isaiah 38:20
see also **Beating, Improvise, Intones,
Played, Player, Playing, Plays, Pluck,
Strike**

Played
1 Samuel 18:7
2 Kings 3:15
Matthew 11:17
Luke 7:32
1 Corinthians 14:7
see also **Beating, Improvise, Intones,
Play, Player, Playing, Plays, Pluck,
Strike**

Player
1 Samuel 16:16
see also **Beating, Improvise, Intones,
Play, Played, Playing, Plays, Pluck,
Strike**

Playing
1 Samuel 18:10
1 Samuel 19:9
1 Kings 1:40
see also **Beating, Improvise, Intones,
Play, Played, Player, Plays, Pluck, Strike**

Plays
Ezekiel 33:32
see also **Beating, Improvise, Intones,
Play, Played, Player, Playing, Pluck,
Strike**

Pluck
Isaiah 23:16
see also **Beating, Improvise, Intones, Play,
Played, Player, Playing, Plays, Strike**

Praise
1 Chronicles 23:5
2 Chronicles 23:13
Ezra 3:10
Psalm 7:17
Psalm 9:2
Psalm 21:13
Psalm 30:12
Psalm 40:3
Psalm 43:4
Psalm 61:8
Psalm 66:2
Psalm 69:30
Psalm 71:22
Psalm 104:33
Psalm 106:12
Psalm 135:3
Psalm 146:2
Psalm 147:1
Psalm 149:1, 3
Psalm 150:3–5
Isaiah 12:5
Jeremiah 20:13
Jeremiah 31:7
Acts 16:25
Romans 15:9
see also **Praise**, **Praised**, **Praises**, **Praising**,
Thanksgiving

Praise
Exodus 15:1–21
Judges 5:1–31
1 Chronicles 16:1–43
1 Chronicles 25:1–31
2 Chronicles 5:11–14
2 Chronicles 7:4–7
2 Chronicles 20:20–30
Nehemiah 12:27–47
see also **Praise**, **Praised**, **Praises**,
Praising, Thanksgiving

Praised
2 Chronicles 30:21
Ezra 3:11

see also **Praise**, Praise, **Praises**, **Praising**,
Thanksgiving

Praises
2 Samuel 22:50
Psalm 9:11
Psalm 18:49
Psalm 27:6
Psalm 33:2
Psalm 47:6–7
Psalm 57:7, 9
Psalm 59:17
Psalm 66:4
Psalm 68:4, 32
Psalm 71:23
Psalm 75:9
Psalm 92:1
Psalm 98:4
Psalm 101:1
Psalm 105:2
Psalm 108:1, 3
Psalm 135:3
Psalm 138:1
Psalm 144:9
Psalm 146:2
Psalm 147:1, 7
Psalm 149:3
James 5:13
see also **Praise**, Praise, **Praised**, **Praising**,
Thanksgiving

Praising
1 Chronicles 23:5
Ezra 3:11
see also **Praise**, Praise, **Praised**, **Praises**,
Thanksgiving

Priests
Joshua 6:1–21
2 Chronicles 5:11–14
2 Chronicles 7:4–7
2 Chronicles 30:21
Ezra 2:1–70
Ezra 3:8–13

Ezra 7:11–26
Nehemiah 12:27–47
Nehemiah 13:4–14

Prophesy
  1 Samuel 10:1–13
  2 Kings 3:13–20
  1 Chronicles 25:1–31

Psalm
  Psalm 3:0
  Psalm 4:0
  Psalm 5:0
  Psalm 6:0
  Psalm 8:0
  Psalm 9:0
  Psalm 11:0
  Psalm 12:0
  Psalm 13:0
  Psalm 14:0
  Psalm 15:0
  Psalm 18:0
  Psalm 19:0
  Psalm 20:0
  Psalm 21:0
  Psalm 22:0
  Psalm 23:0
  Psalm 24:0
  Psalm 25:0
  Psalm 26:0
  Psalm 27:0
  Psalm 28:0
  Psalm 29:0
  Psalm 30:0
  Psalm 31:0
  Psalm 32:0
  Psalm 34:0
  Psalm 35:0
  Psalm 36:0
  Psalm 37:0
  Psalm 38:0
  Psalm 39:0
  Psalm 40:0
  Psalm 41:0

Psalm 46:0
Psalm 47:0, 7
Psalm 48:0
Psalm 49:0
Psalm 50:0
Psalm 51:0
Psalm 61:0
Psalm 62:0
Psalm 63:0
Psalm 64:0
Psalm 65:0
Psalm 66:0
Psalm 67:0
Psalm 68:0
Psalm 69:0
Psalm 70:0
Psalm 72:0
Psalm 73:0
Psalm 75:0
Psalm 76:0
Psalm 77:0
Psalm 79:0
Psalm 80:0
Psalm 81:0
Psalm 82:0
Psalm 83:0
Psalm 84:0
Psalm 85:0
Psalm 87:0
Psalm 88:0
Psalm 92:0
Psalm 98:0
Psalm 100:0
Psalm 101:0
Psalm 103:0
Psalm 108:0
Psalm 109:0
Psalm 110:0
Psalm 138:0
Psalm 139:0
Psalm 140:0
Psalm 141:0
Psalm 143:0
Psalm 144:0

Psalm 145:0
Acts 13:33, 35
1 Corinthians 14:26
see also **Hymn, Hymns, Melody, Psalms,
Song, Songs**

Psalmist
2 Samuel 23:1
see also **Composed, Composition**

Psalms
Psalm 95:2
Luke 20:42
Acts 1:20
Ephesians 5:19
Colossians 3:16
see also **Hymn, Hymns, Melody, Psalm,
Song, Songs**

Psaltery
Daniel 3:5, 7, 10, 15

Ram's horn
Exodus 19:13
Leviticus 25:9

Rams' horns
Joshua 6:4, 6, 8, 13

Resounding
Psalm 92:3
Psalm 150:5

Romamti-Ezer
1 Chronicles 25:4

Sang
Exodus 15:1
Numbers 21:17
Judges 5:1
1 Samuel 18:7
2 Chronicles 20:21
2 Chronicles 29:28, 30
Ezra 3:11
Nehemiah 12:42

Job 38:7
Psalm 7:0
Psalm 106:12
Matthew 11:17
Luke 7:32
Revelation 5:9
Revelation 14:3
Revelation 15:3
see also **Sing, Singer, Singers, Singing,
Sings, Sung**

Saul
1 Samuel 13:3

Selah
Psalm 3:2, 4, 8
Psalm 4:2, 4
Psalm 7:5
Psalm 9:16, 20
Psalm 20:3
Psalm 21:2
Psalm 24:6, 10
Psalm 32:4, 5, 7
Psalm 39:5, 11
Psalm 44:8
Psalm 46:3, 7
Psalm 47:4
Psalm 48:8
Psalm 49:13, 15
Psalm 50:6
Psalm 52:3, 5
Psalm 54:3
Psalm 55:7, 19
Psalm 57:3, 6
Psalm 59:5, 13
Psalm 60:4
Psalm 61:4
Psalm 62:4, 8
Psalm 66:4, 7, 15
Psalm 67:1, 4
Psalm 68:7, 19, 32
Psalm 75:3
Psalm 76:3, 9
Psalm 77:3, 9, 15

Psalm 81:7
Psalm 82:2
Psalm 83:8
Psalm 84:4, 8
Psalm 85:2
Psalm 87:3, 6
Psalm 88:7, 10
Psalm 89:4, 37, 45, 48
Psalm 140:3, 5, 8
Psalm 143:6
Habakkuk 3:3, 9, 13

Sheba
2 Samuel 20:1

Shebaniah
1 Chronicles 15:24

Shebuel
1 Chronicles 25:4

Shemaiah
Nehemiah 12:36, 42

Sheminith
1 Chronicles 15:21

Shemiramoth
1 Chronicles 15:20
1 Chronicles 16:5

Shiggaion
(*dithyrambic rhythm* or
wild, passionate song)
Psalm 7:0

Shimei
1 Chronicles 25:3

Shoshannim
(*lilies*)
Psalm 45:0
Psalm 69:0

Shushan Eduth
(*the lily of testimony*)
Psalm 60:0

Signal
Exodus 19:16
Leviticus 25:9
Numbers 31:6
Joshua 6:1–21
Judges 3:27
Judges 7:1–25
1 Samuel 13:3
2 Samuel 2:28
2 Samuel 15:10
2 Samuel 18:16
2 Samuel 20:1
2 Samuel 20:22
1 Kings 1:32–48
2 Kings 9:13
2 Chronicles 3:4–12
Nehemiah 4:20
Isaiah 5:1
Isaiah 27:13
Jeremiah 4:5, 19
Jeremiah 6:1, 17
Jeremiah 51:27
Ezekiel 33:3–6
Daniel 3:1–18
Hosea 5:8
Hosea 8:1
Joel 2:1, 15
Matthew 6:2
Matthew 24:31
1 Corinthians 14:7, 8
1 Corinthians 15:52
1 Thessalonians 4:16

Sing
Exodus 15:1, 21
Numbers 21:17
Judges 5:3, 10, 12
1 Samuel 21:11
1 Samuel 29:5
2 Samuel 22:50

1 Chronicles 16:9, 33
1 Chronicles 25:6
2 Chronicles 29:30
Job 21:12
Job 29:13
Job 33:27
Psalm 7:17
Psalm 9:2, 11
Psalm 13:6
Psalm 18:49
Psalm 21:13
Psalm 27:6
Psalm 30:12
Psalm 33:2, 3
Psalm 47:6, 7
Psalm 51:14
Psalm 57:7, 9
Psalm 59:16, 17
Psalm 61:8
Psalm 65:13
Psalm 66:2, 4
Psalm 67:4
Psalm 68:4, 32
Psalm 71:22, 23
Psalm 75:9
Psalm 81:1
Psalm 87:7
Psalm 89:1
Psalm 92:1, 4
Psalm 95:1
Psalm 96:1, 2
Psalm 98:1, 4, 5
Psalm 101:1
Psalm 104:33
Psalm 105:2
Psalm 108:1, 3
Psalm 135:3
Psalm 137:3
Psalm 138:1, 5
Psalm 144:9
Psalm 146:2
Psalm 147:1, 7
Psalm 149:1, 3, 5
Ecclesiastes 12:4

Isaiah 5:1
Isaiah 23:16
Isaiah 27:2
Isaiah 42:10, 11
Jeremiah 20:13
Jeremiah 31:7
Hosea 2:15
Zephaniah 2:14
Zechariah 2:10
Romans 15:9
1 Corinthians 14:15
Hebrews 2:12
James 5:13
see also **Sang, Singer, Singers, Singing, Sings, Sung**

Singer
1 Chronicles 6:33
see also **Sang, Sing, Singers, Singing, Sings, Sung**

Singers
1 Kings 10:12
1 Chronicles 9:33
1 Chronicles 15:16, 19, 27
2 Chronicles 5:12, 13
2 Chronicles 9:11
2 Chronicles 23:13
2 Chronicles 29:28
2 Chronicles 35:15, 25
Ezra 2:41, 65, 70
Ezra 7:7, 24
Ezra 10:24
Nehemiah 7:1, 44, 67, 73
Nehemiah 10:28, 39
Nehemiah 11:22
Nehemiah 12:28, 29, 42, 45, 46, 47
Nehemiah 13:5, 10
Psalm 68:25
Ecclesiastes 2:8
Ezekiel 40:44
see also **Sang, Sing, Singer, Singing, Sings, Sung**

(89

Singing
Exodus 32:18
1 Samuel 18:6
2 Samuel 19:35
1 Chronicles 15:22, 27
1 Chronicles 25:7
2 Chronicles 20:22
2 Chronicles 23:18
Ezra 2:65
Psalm 100:2
Matthew 26:30
Mark 14:26
Acts 16:25
Ephesians 5:19
Colossians 3:16
see also **Sang, Sing, Singer, Singers, Sings, Sung**

Sings
Proverbs 25:20
Proverbs 29:6
see also **Sang, Sing, Singer, Singers, Singing, Sung**

Skill
Psalm 137:5
see also Skill, **Skillful, Skillfully**

Skill
Nehemiah 10:28
Ezekiel 33:32
see also **Skill**, Skill, **Skillful, Skillfully**

Skillful
1 Samuel 16:16, 18
1 Chronicles 15:22
1 Chronicles 25:7
2 Chronicles 34:12
Psalm 47:7
see also **Skill**, Skill, **Skillfully**

Skillfully
Psalm 33:3
Isaiah 23:16
see also **Skill**, Skill, **Skillful**

Soloist
Deuteronomy 32:1–43
Judges 11:34
1 Samuel 13:3
1 Samuel 16:14–23
1 Samuel 18:10
1 Samuel 19:9
2 Samuel 18:16
2 Samuel 20:1–22
2 Samuel 22:1–51

Solomon
Nehemiah 12:45
Psalm 72:0
Psalm 127:0
Song of Solomon 1:1

Song
Exodus 15:1, 2
Numbers 21:17
Deuteronomy 31:19, 21, 22, 30
Judges 5:12
2 Samuel 1:18
1 Chronicles 6:31, 32
2 Chronicles 29:27
Psalm 18:0
Psalm 30:0
Psalm 33:3
Psalm 40:3
Psalm 42:8
Psalm 45:0
Psalm 46:0
Psalm 48:0
Psalm 65:0
Psalm 66:0
Psalm 67:0
Psalm 68:0
Psalm 69:12, 30
Psalm 75:0
Psalm 76:0
Psalm 77:6
Psalm 81:2
Psalm 83:0
Psalm 87:0

Psalm 88:0
Psalm 92:0
Psalm 96:1
Psalm 98:1
Psalm 108:0
Psalm 118:14
Psalm 120:0
Psalm 121:0
Psalm 122:0
Psalm 123:0
Psalm 124:0
Psalm 125:0
Psalm 126:0
Psalm 127:0
Psalm 128:0
Psalm 129:0
Psalm 130:0
Psalm 131:0
Psalm 132:0
Psalm 133:0
Psalm 134:0
Psalm 137:4
Psalm 144:9
Psalm 149:1
Ecclesiastes 7:5
Ecclesiastes 12:4
Song of Solomon 1:1
Isaiah 5:1
Isaiah 12:2, 5
Isaiah 23:15
Isaiah 24:9
Isaiah 26:1
Isaiah 30:29
Isaiah 42:10
Lamentations 3:14, 63
Ezekiel 33:32
Habakkuk 2:6
Revelation 5:9
Revelation 14:3
Revelation 15:3
see also **Hymn, Hymns, Melody, Psalm, Psalms, Songs**

Song leaders
Nehemiah 11:23

Songs
Genesis 31:27
1 Kings 4:32
1 Chronicles 13:8
1 Chronicles 16:42
Nehemiah 12:27
Job 35:10
Psalm 32:7
Psalm 119:54
Psalm 137:3
Proverbs 25:20
Song of Solomon 1:1
Isaiah 23:16
Isaiah 24:16
Isaiah 30:29
Isaiah 38:20
Ezekiel 26:13
Amos 5:23
Amos 6:5
Amos 8:3, 10
Ephesians 5:19
Colossians 3:16
see also **Hymn, Hymns, Melody, Psalm, Psalms, Song**

Song text
Exodus 15:1–21
Numbers 21:17
Deuteronomy 32:1–43
Judges 5:1–31
1 Samuel 18:7
1 Samuel 21:11
1 Samuel 29:5
2 Samuel 1:17–27
2 Samuel 3:33–34
2 Samuel 22:1
2 Samuel 23:1–7
1 Chronicles 16:8–36
Ezra 3:10–11
Psalms
Song of Solomon
Isaiah 5:1–30
Isaiah 26:1–21
Habakkuk

Revelation 15:3, 4

Sound
Exodus 19:16, 19
Exodus 20:18
Exodus 32:18
Leviticus 25:9
Numbers 10:9
Joshua 6:5, 20
2 Samuel 6:15
2 Samuel 15:10
1 Kings 1:41
1 Chronicles 15:19, 28
1 Chronicles 16:42
2 Chronicles 13:12
Nehemiah 4:20
Job 21:12
Psalm 47:5
Psalm 98:5, 6
Isaiah 30:29
Isaiah 51:3
Jeremiah 4:19, 21
Jeremiah 6:17
Jeremiah 42:14
Ezekiel 26:13
Ezekiel 33:4, 5
Daniel 3:5, 7, 10, 15
Hosea 5:8
Joel 2:1
Amos 2:2
Amos 5:23
Amos 6:6
Matthew 6:2
1 Corinthians 14:8
Revelation 1:10
Revelation 4:1
Revelation 8:6
Revelation 10:7
Revelation 14:2
Revelation 18:22
see also **Sounded, Sounding, Sounds**

Sounded
2 Chronicles 29:28

Revelation 8:7, 8, 10, 12
Revelation 9:1, 13
Revelation 11:15
see also **Sound, Sounding, Sounds**

Sounding
Numbers 10:7
Psalm 81:2
see also **Sound, Sounded, Sounds**

Sound quality
see **Blast, Clanging, Distinction, Indistinct, Loud-sounding, Noise, Noisy, Resounding, Sweet, Unison, Voice, Wails**

Sounds
Exodus 19:13
Job 39:25
see also **Sound, Sounded, Sounding**

Strike
Psalm 81:2
see also **Beating, Improvise, Intones, Play, Played, Player, Playing, Plays, Pluck**

Stringed instruments
Psalm 4:0
Psalm 6:0
Psalm 54:0
Psalm 55:0
Psalm 61:0
Psalm 67:0
Psalm 76:0
Psalm 150:0
Isaiah 38:20
Habakkuk 3:19

Strings
Isaiah 23:16

Sung
Job 36:24
Isaiah 26:1
see also **Sang, Sing, Singer, Singers,**

Singing, Sings

Support
  Ezra 7:24
  Nehemiah 10:34–39
  Nehemiah 12:44–47
  Nehemiah 13:4–14

Sweet
  2 Samuel 23:1
  Psalm 81:2

Tambourine
  1 Samuel 10:5
  Psalm 68:25
  Isaiah 5:12
see also **Tambourines**

Tambourines
  Judges 11:34
  1 Samuel 18:6
  2 Samuel 6:5
  1 Chronicles 13:8
  Psalm 68:25
  Isaiah 24:8
  Isaiah 30:32
  Jeremiah 31:4
see also **Tambourine**

Taunt-song
  Habakkuk 2:6

Teaching
  Deuteronomy 31:19–22
  2 Samuel 1:18
  1 Chronicles 15:22
  1 Chronicles 25:1–31
  Colossians 3:16

Temple
  2 Kings 12:13

Ten-stringed
  Psalm 92:3

see also **Eight-stringed, Ten strings**

Ten strings
  Psalm 33:2
see also **Eight-stringed, Ten-stringed**

Terms
see **Aijeleth Hashshahar, Alamoth, Al-Tashheth, Ascents, Gittith, Higgaion Selah, Jonath Elem Rehokim, Mahalath, Mahalath Leannoth, Maskil, Mikhtam, Muth-Labben, Selah, Sheminith, Shiggaion, Shoshannim, Shushan Eduth**

Thank
  Psalm 28:7
see also **Thankfulness, Thanks, Thanksgiving**

Thankfulness
  Colossians 3:16
see also **Thank, Thanks, Thanksgiving**

Thanks
  Ezra 3:11
  Psalm 30:12
  Psalm 33:2
  Psalm 57:9
  Psalm 92:1
  Psalm 108:3
  Psalm 138:1
see also **Thanks, Thankfulness, Thanksgiving**

Thanksgiving
  2 Samuel 22:1–51
  1 Chronicles 16:1–43
  Ezra 3:10, 11
  Nehemiah 12:27–47
  Psalm 13:6
  Psalm 33:2, 3
  Psalm 57:7–9
  Psalm 108:1–3

see also **Praise**, Praise, **Praises, Praised, Praising**

Therapy
  1 Samuel 16:14–23
  1 Samuel 18:10–16
  1 Samuel 19:9

Timbrel
  Genesis 31:27
  Exodus 15:20
  Job 21:12
  Psalm 81:2
  Psalm 149:3
  Psalm 150:4
see also **Timbrels**

Timbrels
  Exodus 15:20
see also **Timbrel**

Trigon
  Daniel 3:5, 7, 10, 15
Trumpet
  Exodus 19:16, 19
  Exodus 20:18
  Joshua 6:5, 23
  Judges 6:34
  Judges 7:18
  1 Samuel 13:3
  2 Samuel 2:28
  2 Samuel 6:15
  2 Samuel 15:10
  2 Samuel 18:16
  2 Samuel 20:1, 22
  1 Kings 1:34, 39, 41
  2 Kings 9:13
  Nehemiah 4:20
  Job 39:24, 25
  Psalm 47:5
  Psalm 81:3
  Psalm 150:3
  Isaiah 18:3
  Isaiah 27:13

  Isaiah 58:1
  Jeremiah 4:5, 19, 21
  Jeremiah 6:1, 17
  Jeremiah 42:14
  Jeremiah 51:27
  Ezekiel 7:14
  Ezekiel 33:3–6
  Hosea 5:8
  Hosea 8:1
  Joel 2:1, 15
  Amos 2:2
  Amos 3:6
  Zephaniah 1:16
  Zechariah 9:14
  Matthew 6:2
  Matthew 24:31
  1 Corinthians 15:52
  1 Thessalonians 4:16
  Hebrews 12:19
  Revelation 1:10
  Revelation 4:1
  Revelation 9:14
  Revelation 18:22
see also **Trumpets**

Trumpeter
  Nehemiah 4:18
see also **Trumpeters**

Trumpeters
  2 Kings 11:14
  2 Chronicles 5:13
  2 Chronicles 23:13
  Revelation 18:22
see also **Trumpeter**

Trumpets
  Leviticus 23:24
  Numbers 10:2, 8–10
  Numbers 29:1
  Numbers 31:6
  Joshua 6:4, 6, 8, 9, 13, 16, 20
  Judges 7:8, 16, 18–20, 22
  2 Kings 11:14

2 Kings 12:13
1 Chronicles 13:8
1 Chronicles 15:24, 28
1 Chronicles 16:6, 42
2 Chronicles 5:12, 13
2 Chronicles 7:6
2 Chronicles 13:12, 14
2 Chronicles 15:14
2 Chronicles 20:28
2 Chronicles 23:13
2 Chronicles 29:26–28
Ezra 3:10
Nehemiah 12:35, 41
Psalm 98:6
Revelation 8:2, 6
see also **Trumpet**

Tuned
1 Chronicles 15:20, 21

Unison
2 Chronicles 5:13

Unni
1 Chronicles 15:20

Uzzi
Nehemiah 12:42

Uzziel
1 Chronicles 25:4

Voice
Job 39:24

Wails
Jeremiah 48:36

War
Exodus 15:1–21
Numbers 10:1–10
Numbers 31:1–12
Joshua 6:1–21
Judges 3:26–30

2 Chronicles 13:14
Job 39:24, 25
Isaiah 30:27–33
Isaiah 38:10–20
Jeremiah 4:19–22

Warnings
Exodus 32:18, 19
Isaiah 5:11, 12
Isaiah 23:16
Amos 5:23
Amos 6:5
Job 21:12, 13

Witness
Deuteronomy 31:19–22
Joshua 6:1–21
Psalm 9:11
Psalm 40:3
Psalm 51:14
Psalm 57:7, 9
Psalm 59:16, 17
Psalm 66:2, 4
Psalm 67:4
Psalm 68:4
Psalm 69:30
Psalm 75:9, 10
Psalm 89:1
Psalm 92:1–4
Psalm 96:1, 2
Psalm 98:1
Psalm 137:2–4
Psalm 138:5
Psalm 149:1, 5
Isaiah 12:1–6

Women
Exodus 15:20, 21
Judges 5:1–31
1 Samuel 18:6–9
2 Samuel 19:35
Ezra 2:65
Nehemiah 7:67
Psalm 68:25

Ecclesiastes 2:8
Ecclesiastes 12:4

Worship
Psalm 66:4
Isaiah 27:13
Daniel 3:5, 10, 15
see also Worship

Worship
Exodus 32:18
Nehemiah 12:27–47
1 Corinthians 14:26
see also **Worship**

Worshiped
2 Chronicles 29:30
Daniel 3:7

Zaccur
1 Chronicles 25:2

Zechariah
1 Chronicles 15:20, 24
1 Chronicles 16:5
2 Chronicles 34:12
Nehemiah 12:41
Zeri
1 Chronicles 25:3